Wisdom from Proverbs:

Devotions for

Homeschooling Moms

by Barbara Coyle

Dedication

To my husband, Tim, who is so enthusiastic about my role
as a homeschooling mom,

To my mother, who would have homeschooled me if such a
thing had been thought of back then, and who exemplifies
so many of the virtues found in these Proverbs,

And to Lois Green, my fellow missionary homeschooling
mom, who has encouraged me so much by her example as a
true Proverbs 31 woman.

Preface

This devotional book grew out of my own studies in the book of Proverbs. These verses have convicted, challenged, and encouraged me in my journey as a homeschooling wife and mother. I have not yet learned all they have to teach me, and these devotionals were written for my sake even more than anyone else's.

If God uses one of the verses in this book to convict you of an area of your life that you need to change, I encourage you memorize that verse and also some of the verses listed at the end of that devotional. After all, "Your word I have hidden in my heart, that I might not sin against You" (Psalm 119:11). Having God's word memorized will be a great help in overcoming the sins that hinder us in running the race.

However, many moms have difficulty finding the time for memorization, or they forget to review the verses they've learned. There are many Bible memory systems available, and many hints and ideas that could work for your family. Here is one idea that has worked for our family: at mealtimes, just before we ask God's blessing on the food, we say the Bible verse together as a family. We type it up in large print and post it somewhere where the readers in the family can see it from the table. After two weeks, we all know the verse! We often say two verses before dinner: one "review" verse, and one that we're learning. We just change the "review" verse every few days.

Think about it: you still know the Pledge of Allegiance, don't you? How did you learn that? By repeating it every day. If you repeat it enough times, you won't forget it. Then God's word will be in your heart, instantly available for the Holy Spirit to use in your life.

God bless you as you study the riches of His word!

Barbara Coyle
Enybegs, Co. Longford
Ireland

Note: All Scriptures quoted are from the New King James Version

1

Let not mercy and truth forsake you; bind them around your neck, write them on the tablet of your heart, and so find favor and high esteem in the sight of God and man. Proverbs 3:3, 4

The word "mercy" here could also be translated "kindness" or even "loving-kindness." Among other things, it means to be gentle, considerate, amiable, congenial and sympathetic. What would our homes be like if those character qualities never left us? Picture a mother who has had very little sleep. She awakens to one child who is out of sorts and grumpy, a mess that wasn't cleaned up properly by the person responsible, a baby who is irritable because of illness, and a husband who needs her to help him that morning with something. Is it possible for such a mother to respond to it all with gentleness, sympathy, and kindness? Yes, it is, but only with God's help.

Loving-kindness is more than just reactive, though. It is also pro-active. It reaches out. As we serve our families, mercy can take the form of planning or making something special for our husband or children. It can be remembering to show affection to our children, even when we don't feel particularly affectionate. It can be showing sympathy to anyone in the family who is having a difficult time.

Mercy should be so much a part of our character that it also shows itself to those outside our family. Would your in-laws characterize you as someone who is full of kindness? What about people at church or the salespeople you encounter while running errands? Even if they disagree with your lifestyle choices, would they still have to admit that you are a kind person?

Often it takes very little for our mercy and kindness to flee. Sometimes just being tired is enough for a mom to let mercy forsake her. So how do we make mercy such a part of our lives that even when we are tempted to be irritable and angry, by God's grace we will have mercy staying with us?

The first thing we can do is to pray about it. Ask God to show you when you are beginning to lose your attitude of mercy, and then ask for His help to get it back. Meditate on the character of Jesus, and ask God to make you like Him.

Another thing we can do is to memorize Scripture that pertains to this issue. Better yet, teach these verses to your children as well. It will help you remember them better, and you will have more accountability to live them out!

For further study:

I Corinthians 13:1-13 Though I speak with the tongues of men and of angels, but have not love, I have become sounding brass or a clanging cymbal. And though I have the gift of prophecy, and understand all mysteries and all knowledge, and though I have all faith, so that I could remove mountains, but have not love, I am nothing. And though I bestow all my goods to feed the poor, and though I give my body to be burned, but have not love, it profits me nothing. Love suffers long and is kind; love does not envy; love does not parade itself, is not puffed up; does not behave rudely, does not seek its own, is not provoked, thinks no evil; does not rejoice in iniquity, but rejoices in the truth; bears all things, believes all things, hopes all things, endures all things. Love never fails. But whether there are prophesies, they will fail; whether there are tongues, they will cease; whether there is knowledge, it will vanish away. And now abide faith, hope, love, these three; but the greatest of these is love.

Luke 6:37 Judge not, and you shall not be judged. Condemn not, and you shall not be condemned. Forgive, and you will be forgiven.

Colossians 3:12 Therefore, as the elect of God, holy and beloved, put on tender mercies, kindness, humility, meekness, longsuffering.

2

Let not mercy and truth forsake you; Bind them around your neck, write them on the tablet of your heart, and so find favor and high esteem in the sight of God and man. Proverbs 3:3, 4

Last time we thought about the word "mercy" in these verses. Today let us consider the word "truth."

I remember when I realized that I was in the habit of telling a particular lie to my preschool-aged son. It would happen when he started to ask questions and the questions got difficult to answer (or I knew that answering that one question would mean answering several more). Rather than think about how I could answer him, I took the easiest way out and said, "I don't know."

Now, there are times when I really *don't* know, and then this is an acceptable answer. And there are times when he doesn't need to have that question answered, and he can be told that, too. But in these situations, I was just being lazy, and was willing to lie to end the conversation quickly.

There are so many situations that tempt us to be less than truthful. Do you habitually tell your children you will do something for them, and then never get around to it? If you advertise something to sell, is your description of it strictly accurate? Some homeschoolers who live in a place that requires them to record how many hours of homeschooling they do every day find it very easy to "round-up" the minutes to the next hour, or count an activity as an "educational opportunity" that no educator would consider as such. Telling "little" lies for the sake of convenience is a very easy habit to get into. And once you have that habit, it is sometimes hard for you to catch yourself telling them: you begin to lie without even being consciously aware that you are lying!

God is described in the book of Titus as the God "who cannot lie" (Titus 1:2). Literally, it means "the non-lying kind of God." Truthfulness is an intrinsic part of the character of God, and he hates any kind of falsehood. If you are in the habit of lying, you need to repent. Pray that God will make you aware of when you are lying, and purpose in your heart not to tell another lie.

For further study:

Exodus 20:16 "You shall not bear false witness against your neighbor."

Isaiah 59:2, 3 "But your iniquities have separated you from your God; and your sins have hidden His face from you, so that He will not hear. For your hands are defiled with blood, and your fingers with iniquity; your lips have spoken lies, your tongue has muttered perversity."

Psalm 119:63 "I am a companion of all who fear You, and of those who keep Your precepts."

3

Better is the poor who walks in his integrity than one perverse in his ways, though he be rich. Proverbs 28:6

It is always a temptation for the poor to be less than honest. When we don't have enough money, we can justify to ourselves many little deceptions. I have known Christian women who fudged a little to get a bigger discount, or to take advantage of a special offer that, strictly, they had no right to. I have known them to copy material that was copyrighted because they couldn't afford to buy the copies they wanted. Some families aren't strictly honest when it comes time to report deductions from their income tax. And the world of digital video and music files offers immense temptations to copy or download an illegal copy instead of buying your own.

What does it mean to have integrity? It means that you are innocent of any wrongdoing, and that your character is stainless. It means to be like Daniel, whose enemies looked long and hard at his life for anything they could accuse him of, and couldn't find anything. They actually had to make something he was doing right into a crime in order to get him! If someone looked at your life the way these enemies of Daniel's did at his, would they be able to fault you at any point?

If you struggle with honesty, meditate on Psalm 101:7 "He who works deceit shall not dwell within my house; He who tells lies shall not continue in my presence." We see that King David took this sin so seriously that he would not tolerate anyone who practiced it. And if David takes such a serious view of it, what does God think?

If you cheat and deceive because you think your poverty entitles you to do so, what you are saying is that God is not able to take care of you if you obey Him. You are trying to "help" him provide for you by disobeying Him. What a lack of faith and trust in God! Is the omnipotent God of the universe, who made everything and owns everything, depending on our disobedience to have our needs taken care of? How absurd!

Though this verse is a challenge to us, it is also a comfort. If we are poor and still have integrity, we have higher worth and nobility than those who are wealthy but dishonest. In the eyes of God, there is nothing shameful about poverty. Very few of the people that God has greatly used throughout history have been rich; most of them could be classified as poor. I'd rather be in their company, wouldn't you? Whatever level of income God has ordained for us right now, let us live in a way that honors Him!

For further study:

Isaiah 29:19 "The humble also shall increase their joy in the Lord, and the poor among men shall rejoice in the Holy One of Israel.

James 1:9 "Let the lowly brother glory in his exaltation, but the rich in his humiliation, because as a flower of the field he will pass away."

Proverbs 19:1 "Better is the poor who walks in his integrity than one who is perverse in his lips, and is a fool."

4

Make no friendship with an angry man, and with a furious man do not go, lest you learn his ways and set a snare for your soul. Proverbs 22:24, 25

The message of these verses is simple: stay away from an angry person, or it will rub off on you, and be a stumbling block for you. In our home, we separate an angry child from his siblings, so they will not learn his ways.

However, have you ever considered that if you are angry, it is almost impossible for your children to obey this verse? They can hardly banish you to your room until you repent, nor can they usually remove themselves from your presence. They are stuck with an angry person. And they will, no doubt, learn your ways and set a snare for their souls. What about your husband? He may not have to spend as much time with you as your children do, but he certainly has a "friendship" with you, and you will influence him with your anger.

I have yet to meet a wife and mother who doesn't struggle with anger in some degree. A pastor once told my husband, "I thought I was a very patient person until I got married and had children!" Something about marriage and parenthood brings out more exasperated feelings than we thought we were capable of! Of course, all this sin was in our hearts before: it just took the right circumstances to show it to us. One of the blessings of family life is that God can use it to mature us and make us more like His Son.

We all know that screaming at our children, slamming doors, and giving our husbands "the silent treatment" is wrong. We may not feel as guilty about a frustrated tone of voice, a sharp answer to a question, or an angry action (closing the car door a little more firmly than is necessary!). But they are all wrong, and all likely to lead to a snare for the souls of those that are close to us.

Oh dear sister, when you consider what is at stake, will you not cry out to God for His deliverance from anger? You *can* be delivered from it! God can give us the power to overcome any sin, and that includes anger.

For further study:

James 1:19-20 "So then, my beloved brethren, let every man be swift to hear, slow to speak, slow to wrath; for the wrath of man does not produce the righteousness of God."

Philippians 4:5 "Let your gentleness be known to all men. The Lord is at hand."

Colossians 3:8 "But now you yourselves are to put off all these: anger, wrath, malice, blasphemy, filthy language out of your mouth."

5

Go to the ant, you sluggard! Consider her ways and be wise, which, having no captain, overseer or ruler, provides her supplies in the summer, and gathers her food in the harvest. Proverbs 6:6-8

For most homeschooling mothers, the battle against laziness is an ongoing one. I have been part of an internet forum for homeschooling moms for several years, and over and over I read statements like this: "I just can't seem to keep our family on a schedule. I know the benefits of having an ordered life, and when we are on schedule, our whole family loves it. But I just don't seem to have the self-discipline to make it happen consistently." Other moms mention how they hate to do dishes or laundry, and so it all piles up and they feel overwhelmed.

There is some benefit in having accountability with your husband, or another woman, until you overcome the bad habits of laziness. But the best motivation is internal. The writer of Proverbs here instructs us to look at the ant, who works hard without any overseer making sure he does. Accountability will, at some point, fail us. It is a crutch that we can use if we can't do it on our own, but eventually we will either build good habits and not need the crutch, or the crutch will break and we will be back where we were. If you require accountability to keep yourself on the right path in a certain area, then work toward becoming self-motivated with God as your main accountability.

The ant is also commended for gathering food in the summer and harvest times, to store up for winter. We need to be industrious doing whatever the season we are in requires. A mom on strict bedrest, for example, can hardly be faulted for having a less-than-spotless house! This is a season of life not conducive to organizing the house and holding a garage sale, going on homeschool field trips, or helping with Vacation Bible School! However, it would be a good season for her to spend more time in prayer and Bible reading, writing notes to those who need encouragement, planning for homeschooling lessons, planning for *anything*, and doing needlework. But the harder she worked while she was able to, the easier the bedrest season of her life will be. For example, the children will be trained to help with the running of the house (as much as their abilities will allow them to), perhaps there will be meals already made and frozen to be prepared easily, and the home will be fairly uncluttered and easier to keep tidy.

In learning to work diligently, we are working against our flesh, and possibly also against the habits of a lifetime! May God give us strength to do what He has called us to, and also a vision for the blessings that come from hard work.

For further study:

Colossians 3:23, 24 "And whatever you do, do it heartily, as to the Lord and not to men, knowing that from the Lord you will receive the reward of the inheritance; for you serve the Lord Christ."

Romans 12:11 "Not lagging in diligence, fervent in spirit, serving the Lord"

Ecclesiastes 10:18 "Because of laziness the building decays, and through idleness of hands the house leaks."

6

Anxiety in the heart of man causes depression, but a good word makes it glad. Proverbs 12:25

We want our husbands and children to have glad hearts, don't we? A woman with a depressed husband or child feels her heart burdened and aching until they are joyful again.

However, we could contribute to anxiety and depression in our families without even knowing it! A man can be burdened down with anxiety because he has a wife who lectures, criticizes or ignores him when he makes a mistake or does something she doesn't like. If he is coming home late from work, he may dread coming in the house to hear her barrage of words: "How come you're late? Didn't you think to call me? Dinner's been ready for half an hour! Are you going to make a habit of this?"

My husband is a very intelligent man, but he often has his mind on two things at once. Sometimes he asks me a question and hears my reply, but it doesn't really register in his mind. A minute later he will ask me the same question, and sometimes even ask a third or fourth time in the space of a few minutes! This used to cause me to get annoyed with him. I would think up sarcastic little replies, or say in an irritated voice, "Like I said *four times already*...." One day it occurred to me that he wasn't doing it on purpose. Furthermore, I didn't want him to have to be so worried about my bad reaction that he would have to stop and think about *every* little question he asked me and whether he had asked it before. This would cause him anxiety, and would certainly lead to being downcast in his heart. I can't say that I have never since reacted poorly to being asked something twice, but I can say that I have improved!

Does your husband have to tiptoe around you during certain times of the month because he isn't sure what will set you off? Do your children hesitate when answering your questions, because the wrong answer will result in a long, unpleasant tirade? Or are they afraid of confessing wrong, because you will withhold your affection from them for a while?

Instead of causing anxiety for our loved ones, we need to be in the habit of giving out "good words." These are words of encouragement, love, and hope. When our husband has made a mistake, we can offer him hope that God will use even his mistakes for His glory and purposes. We can encourage our child that we love him no matter what he has done, and that any consequences we may mete out for his wrongdoing are as a result of our love for him and our desire to see him trained in godly ways. When a family member is discouraged by something other than sin, we can express our support of him or her, and even pray with them about the situations. These kinds of good words truly make the heart glad.

For further study:

I Corinthians 13:7 "[Love] bears all things, believes all things, hopes all things; endures all things."

Ephesians 4:29 "Let no corrupt word proceed out of your mouth, but what is good for necessary edification, that it may impart grace to the hearers."

Colossians 4:6 "Let your speech always be with grace, seasoned with salt, that you may know how you ought to answer each one."

7

Correct your son, and he will give you rest; yes, he will give delight to your soul.
Proverbs 29:17

I remember hearing a homeschooling mother say that she was finding it so hard to school her children because they were fighting her every step of the way. She couldn't get them to do their work, she couldn't get them to leave each other alone, and she couldn't keep them from interrupting her when she was trying to work with another child. I remember the frustration and a sense of despair in her words: "How are they ever going to learn anything?"

I'm sure all homeschooling moms have moments and days like this woman was describing. But if it is a continual pattern, where day after day they won't do as you ask them to do, then you have a discipline problem. This verse tells us that a child who is disciplined will give us rest and delight. The word "correct" here means to correct in such a way that there is a change in the child's behaviour.

There are some wonderful, biblical books on parenting available. I have read several of them and have been greatly helped by the wisdom in their pages. Sometimes, however, I fail to correct my children when I should because I am lazy. I am valuing my rest at the moment more than I value the rest that will ultimately come to me when my child is consistently obedient.

There are many biblical motivations for correcting our children. We need to do it because God has commanded it (Ephesians 6:4), because we are concerned about the state of their hearts and want to help them change (Proverbs 22:15), and because it will be a blessing to them if they are obeying us (Ephesians 6:3). But here the writer of Proverbs gives us a reason that benefits us directly—we will be the recipients of rest and delight.

Aside from all the other excellent reasons to discipline our children when they do wrong, wouldn't it be a great help to your homeschool if you had children who obeyed you immediately, completely, and pleasantly? Wouldn't there be a sense of rest in your home, even during times of work, because there was an atmosphere of calm? It is worth it! If you don't know how to discipline your children biblically, then do some research. Read your Bible. Pray. Ask trusted counsellors for suggestions of biblically-based books on training children. And then go forward, with your eyes on all the blessings God gives to those who follow His instructions.

Eph. 6:1-4 "Children, obey your parents in the Lord, for this is right. Honor your father and mother, which is the fist commandment with promise: that it may be well with you and you may live long on the earth. And you, fathers, do not provoke your children to wrath, but bring them up in the training and admonition of the Lord."

Proverbs 22:6 "Train up a child in the way he should go, and when he is old he will not depart from it."

Proverbs 22:15 "Foolishness is bound up in the heart of a child; the rod of correction will drive it far from him."

8

A fool's wrath is known at once, but a prudent man covers shame. Proverbs 12:16

Have you ever had someone make a snide remark about the number of children you have? ("Don't you know what causes that?") Has someone ever made a comment that showed they assumed you were unintelligent because you were a stay at home mother? ("Those of us that have been to college....") Or have you been accused of depriving your children of a happy childhood? ("But they won't be *normal* if you don't send them to school!") These kinds of comments can make our blood boil! Someone once made a comment about our children that I am still tempted to be angry and bitter over.

If the person who makes the comment is a relative, sometimes we have an even harder time keeping our temper under control. We can think of all kinds of clever comebacks and brood over how ridiculous their accusations are. We can expend much energy mentally arguing with them and refuting their allegations, and all the while, bitterness is growing up in our hearts.

As difficult as these comments are to endure, we should follow the advice given in this proverb. It labels us as fools if we make known our anger when we are insulted. A passionate defence of ourselves is always a bad idea. On the other hand, this verse says that a prudent or wise man ignores the offence.

I Corinthians 13:5 says that love "does not behave rudely," and "is not provoked." It takes an enormous measure of self-control not to speak up when you feel under attack! It is something we need to prepare our hearts for beforehand, because often the attack comes unexpectedly and we react before we have time to think it through. What are some kind and Christ-honoring words you could use if you are offended? How could you turn the conversation or end it sweetly without entering into a debate? As you may have learned, debating on any issue where the other person is convinced they are right and you are wrong rarely does anything but provoke more arguments. Your sweetness of speech and gentleness of manner may do more to bring them around to your viewpoint than any amount of evidence you have that you are correct.

If you need a real-life example of this in action, consider the life of Christ: "Who, when he was reviled, did not revile in return; when He suffered, He did not threaten, but committed Himself to Him who judges righteously" (I Peter 2:23).

For further study:

Psalm 37:8 "Cease from anger, and forsake wrath; do not fret—it only causes harm."

Romans 12:19 "Beloved, do not avenge yourselves, but rather give place to wrath; for it is written, 'Vengeance is Mind, I will repay,' says the Lord."

Ephesians 4:32 "Let no corrupt word proceed out of your mouth, but what is good for necessary edification, that it may impart grace to the hearers."

9

He who is of a proud heart stirs up strife, but he who trusts in the Lord will be prospered.
Proverbs 28:25

One aspect of pride is that it thinks it deserves whatever it wants to have. We can picture some wealthy, famous person thinking "I deserve to have the best because I am the greatest!" It's easy to label that kind of statement as pride. However, we can fall into exactly that same sort of pride without even recognizing it as such.

Have you ever considered what it is that you feel you deserve? Most of us know the Bible well enough that we wouldn't glibly say, "Oh, I *deserve* a good life with no worries, obedient children, and a loving husband." But did you know that unconsciously you probably do think you deserve those things?

Why is it that we get so irritated when a child disobeys or forgets to do what he should? Most of the time it is because we are inconvenienced by his wrongdoing, and we feel that he has violated our right to be free of difficulties at that moment. Why do we get upset with our husbands if we feel they are being selfish? Probably because we think we have a right to be treated with selfless devotion. My husband once observed that he gets frustrated with traffic jams because deep down he really believes he has the right to an easy car journey.

The Bible tells us that all we really deserve is Hell. (Romans 6:23) That means that we don't just deserve Hell at the end of our lives, but we deserve to be in Hell *right now*! When we begin to grasp the enormity of what Christ has done in rescuing us from our lost condition, we will truly have a humble heart. We will not think that we deserve anything; we will just be grateful for our salvation. And then when we realize that He has also given us so many blessings on top of that, we will have a thankful, content heart that is not concerned at all about our "rights" and what we think we need or deserve.

In our quest for the gracious, sweet attitude that God wants us to have, let us clothe ourselves with humility (I Peter 5:5).

For further study:

Philippians 2:3,4 "Let nothing be done through selfish ambition or conceit, but in lowliness of mind let each esteem others better than himself. Let each of you look out not only for his own interests, but also for the interests of others."

Matthew 20:26-28 "Yet it shall not be so among you; but whoever desires to become great among you, let him be your servant. And whoever desires to become great among you, let him be your servant. And whoever desires to be first among you, let him be your slave—just as the Son of Man did not come to be served, but to serve, and to give His life a ransom for many."

10

The simple believes every word, but the prudent considers well his steps. Proverbs 14:15

Before I was married I taught English, and had my students write research papers. I was sometimes amazed at the sources they quoted in all good faith. For many people, the fact that something is published gives it credibility, and they assume it is true. Since I have been at home and homeschooling, I have noticed the same gullibility in homeschooling circles. Some women make decisions about vaccination, Bible versions, circumcising baby boys, or whether or not to use soy products solely based on one article about it that they found on the internet.

I can tell you that many "researched" books and articles—ones that cite scientific studies done on the topic and ones that have tons of referenced works—are not solid research at all. It is especially easy to swallow these if they reinforce a view that you already had. Some authors misquote their sources (purposely, it seems, because it is so blatant) and others just don't take into account other research that might give another view.

If an issue is important to you, research it thoroughly. Read opposing arguments. Look up the sources that are quoted. Pray about it. Even if it is an author who you know to be right on many issues, consider each issue on its own. If you don't do this, the Bible calls you "simple" or naïve. This is not a compliment! It is another way of expressing that you are a fool.

I have many times been embarrassed by Christians who made statements in public which showed that they really didn't have a grasp of the issues, or had gotten hold of some obviously incorrect information. No wonder the world often ridicules us for being ignorant! Our testimony should be that we are prudent and wise…that we can't be taken in easily.

We need to teach this virtue to our children, too. When they are doing research, they need to think their sources through carefully. They need to read through history textbooks—even Christian ones—knowing that they are not infallible. They need to learn that "a good article" is more than just one that promotes something you agree with. May God help us to stop being simple-minded, gullible people, and be prudent and wise in the way we form our opinions.

For further study:

Proverbs 18:17 "The first one to plead his cause seems right, until his neighbor comes and examines him."

Psalm 19:13 "Keep back Your servant also from presumptuous sins; let them not have dominion over me. Then I shall be blameless, and I shall be innocent of great transgression."

11

A sound heart is life to the body, but envy is rottenness to the bones. Proverbs 14:30

Envy is something God hates. James 3:16 says, "For where envy and self-seeking exist, confusion and every evil thing are there." Notice that envy and self-seeking go together: selfishness is at the root of envy. These sins often lead to other ones like bitterness, covetousness, anger, anxiety, and rebellion. You can see why I Peter 2:1 urges us to lay aside all envy!

A woman can be tempted to be envious in many different situations.

- She can be jealous that her husband does not seem to work as hard as she does, and envious of the amount of free time he has.
- She can be envious of someone else's family life—perhaps the other woman's husband is more of a spiritual leader and more godly than her own husband is.
- She can envy another family's income.
- She can be jealous of the attention and praise someone else gets for doing the same ministry she does.
- She can be envious of another woman's fertility...or else of her smaller family.

And you can think of many more examples, I'm sure! The verse in Proverbs that we are looking at says that envy is rottenness to the bones. Aside from all the spiritual calamities that come upon an envious heart, it is also not good for your body! Jealousy and bitterness will eat away at your health.

But there is an antidote to envy. The verse contrasts a jealous heart with a "sound heart." The words "sound heart" could also be translated "quiet and stable heart." It means a heart that is content with the life God has blessed you with. A heart like this is healthy for you not only in the spiritual realm, but also in the physical arena of health. How do we learn to be content? Hebrews 13:5 helps us here: "Let your conduct be without covetousness; be content with such things as you have. For He Himself has said, "I will never leave you or forsake you." We learn to be content by looking at our lives from God's perspective. God thinks that if you have Him, you have enough. The fact that He will never leave or forsake us should be enough to make us content. What does it matter if our circumstances aren't to our liking? We have *God*! And we know that He has planned out every detail of our lives, according to His will.

Hebrews 13:15 "Therefore by Him let us continually offer the sacrifice of praise to God, that is, the fruit of our lips, giving thanks to His name."

Psalm 73:2, 3, 12-18, 25, 26 "But as for me, my feet had almost stumbled; my steps had nearly slipped. For I was envious of the boastful, when I saw the prosperity of the wicked...Behold these are the ungodly, who are always at ease; they increase in riches. Surely I have cleansed my heart in vain, and washed my hands in innocence. For all day long I have been plagued, and chastened every morning. If I had said, 'I will speak thus,' behold, I would have been untrue to the generation of Your children. When I thought how to understand this, it was too painful for me — until I went into the sanctuary of God; then I understood their end. Surely You set them in slippery places; You cast them down to destruction...Whom have I in heaven but You? And there is none upon earth that I desire besides You. My flesh and my heart fail; but God is the strength of my heart and my portion forever.

(If you can, get your Bible and read the whole Psalm.)

12

How long will you slumber, O sluggard? When will you rise from your sleep? A little sleep, a little slumber, a little folding of the hands to sleep – so shall your poverty come on you like a prowler, and your need like an armed man. Proverbs 6:9-11

I heard once of a study conducted to see what mothers of young children craved most. The answer was *sleep*. Certainly we are more likely to be at our best in every area of life if we are rested. This verse is not saying that we should feel guilty if we are trying to get proper rest. The verse is condemning the sluggard who neglects his responsibilities by indulging himself in more rest than is needed. This application could be broadened to include any unnecessary comfort that we indulge in at the expense of our real duties. Homeschooling moms can spend hours watching TV or videos (even educational things like a history channel), browsing on the internet, or reading books. If you are doing what you *desire* to do instead of what you *need* to do, then this verse is a warning to you.

The verse highlights the excuse that is common to every sluggard: "A little sleep, a little slumber, a little folding of the hands to sleep…" We might say, "I'll just hit the snooze button one more time" …. "I'm just going to watch this one show, and then I'll turn the TV off"…."I just want to look up this one thing online"… But the verse makes it clear that the sluggard is not just indulging in a "little slumber," but sleeping a lot more than he needs to! The I'll-just-be-online-for-five-minutes excuse is rarely accurate. Half an hour later you're still surfing the internet.

But there are consequences for the sluggard's behaviour. It says here that your "poverty [will] come on you like a prowler, and your need like an armed man." That is, the penalty for your sloth will be unexpected and devastating. It might be literal poverty, as you neglect household finance issues like paying bills and being a good steward of what you have. It might be the loss of your husband's respect, or that of your children, the loss of a good testimony to those outside the faith, or the loss of opportunity to minister to others in the church. Certainly, your children will miss out on the kind of education they could have, if you were diligent. And their work ethic will suffer, too: it is impossible to teach children to work hard with a good attitude if you yourself are a sluggard!

The next time you catch yourself thinking, "I'll just indulge myself in this for a few minutes," remember this passage of Scripture, and heed its warning!

For further study:

Proverbs 18:9 "He who is slothful in his work is a brother to him who is a great destroyer."

I Corinthians 4:2 "Moreover it is required in stewards that one be found faithful."

Proverbs 10:26 " As vinegar to the teeth and smoke to the eyes, so is the lazy man to those who send him."

13

In the multitude of words sin is not lacking, but he who restrains his lips is wise.
Proverbs 10:19

You've probably heard the sermon anecdote about the man who described his wife as one who spoke an average of 450 words per hour, with gusts up to 580! Women do like to talk! But as this verse tells us, it is dangerous to talk too much. You can't help but sin with your mouth if you never stop talking. Jesus said that the things that proceed out of our mouths come from the heart. If our hearts are less than perfect, our speech will be less than perfect, too. It is true that keeping our mouths shut so that the sin in our hearts doesn't come out won't solve the real sin issues of our lives. But the consequences of our sin will be worse if we not only have to deal with our sinful hearts but also the consequences of our careless speech!

There may be sin in too many words even if what we are saying has no inherent evil in it. We may be insensitive in talking too much, not allowing the other person to share what they're thinking. I know that I've been guilty of using the time the other person is talking only to plan out what I'm going to say next!

Where I live, there are hardly any other homeschooling families. The other day I had a chance to talk to a homeschooling mother, and I felt like we had so much in common. Unwisely, I started talking to the woman as if she were a bosom friend. I went into great detail about all our homeschooling theories, and my personal feelings on every aspect of our lifestyle. I made what were meant to be humorous little statements, and commented on the trials of being surrounded by people who don't understand. She was very friendly and sweet, and never once looked bored at my recital. But later that night I recalled some of the things that I had said. I realized that my little jokes might have been taken differently than I meant them, and that though I felt at the time I was truly sharing my heart about feeling alone, I might have been merely complaining. What might have been appropriate to say to a truly close friend wasn't appropriate to say to someone I'd just met! I would have done well to heed this verse, and restrain my lips a little. Once you've said your words, you can't take them back again!

The good news is that we can train ourselves to have good habits of speech just as we might have trained ourselves in bad habits. We can learn to pause and *think* before making a statement or answering a question. Ask the Holy Spirit to remind you of the truth of this verse the next time words are gushing out of your mouth!

For further study:

Proverbs 13:3 "He who guards his mouth preserves his life, but he who opens wide his lips shall have destruction."

Proverbs 15:28 "The heart of the righteous studies how to answer, but the mouth of the wicked pours forth evil."

Philippians 1:9 "And this I pray, that your love may abound still more and more in knowledge and all discernment."

14

Happy is the man who is always reverent, but he who hardens his heart will fall into calamity. Proverbs 28:14

I started off my college years at a wonderful Christian college. I remember one of the college leaders saying to us assembled freshmen, "While you are at this college, you will be overwhelmed with sermons, information, and studies about the Bible. By the time you graduate, you will have trained yourself either to hear God's Word and obey it, or to hear God's Word and ignore it. It is a dangerous thing to be trained to ignore God's Word."

In all likelihood, you are also surrounded by Scripture. You probably attend at least one church service a week, and that may be supplemented with another Bible study, family devotions, personal devotions, sermon tapes, and/or Bible as a school subject that you teach to your children. What is your attitude while you are hearing the Word of God taught? Are you hungry for the truth, because you want to apply it to your life? Do you mentally critique the sermon or lesson? Does your mind wander to how you're going to get your daughter past long division or what you will serve when that family comes for dinner next week? Do you apply the sermon…to everyone else in your life, but not to yourself?

To harden your heart means that your mind is closed to receiving what God has to say to you. It is no surprise that a person with a hard heart comes to calamity! We ignore God at our peril. "Do not harden your hearts, as in the rebellion, as in the day of trial in the wilderness, when your fathers tested Me; They tried Me, though they saw My work. For forty years I was grieved with that generation and said, 'It is a people who go astray in their hearts, and they do not know my ways. So I swore in My wrath, they shall not enter My rest.'" (Psalm 95:8-11)

On the other hand, someone who always reveres God and listens to what He says will be happy. "But on this one will I look: on him who is poor and of a contrite spirit, and who trembles at My word." (Isaiah 66:2b)

Hebrews 12:28 "Therefore, since we are receiving a kingdom which cannot be shaken, let us have grace, by which we may serve God acceptably with reverence and godly fear."

Deuteronomy 13:4 "You shall walk after the Lord your God and fear Him, and keep his commandments and obey His voice; you shall serve Him and hold fast to Him."

Job 28:28 "And to man He said, 'Behold, the fear of the Lord, that is wisdom, and to depart from evil is understanding.'"

15

Trust in the Lord with all your heart, and lean not on your own understanding.
Proverbs 3:5

Whole-hearted trust in the Lord should be our goal. A woman who trusts in the Lord with her whole heart has full confidence in Him. In what areas do we need to trust the Lord?

1. We need to trust that God is in control of all things in our lives. Nothing is outside of His control or power.
2. We need to trust that God is both wise and kind; in short, we need to trust that God's character is what He says it is in His Word.
3. We need to trust that obeying God in all things really is the best way.

Christian women often have doubts about all these areas. We sometimes are tempted to think that God is not in control of some things—another person's sin, for example, or the interruptions in our daily schedule. Or we feel that although God is in control of a situation, He is being cruel to us. How could a kind God want us to go through infertility, the fatal illness of a child, severe financial difficulties, or marriage problems? And sometimes we excuse our sin to ourselves because we think it's not really a big deal. We say to ourselves, "I'll have to work on this weakness of mine....next week." But all these ways of thinking are contrary to Scripture, and unworthy of the God whom we were saved to worship.

The next part of the verse says that we are not to lean on our own understanding. The book of Proverbs has a lot to say about understanding: "Happy is the man who finds wisdom, and the man who gains understanding" (3:13) is just one of many verses that urge us to obtain understanding. But if we *trust* in our understanding, it will fail us. Depending on ourselves is a failing common to mankind, and God told the prophet Jeremiah that His people had done just that. "For My people have committed two evils: they have forsaken Me, the fountain of living waters, and hewn for themselves cisterns—broken cisterns that can hold no water" (2:13). When we lean on our own understanding

34

instead of God's, we inevitably exchange that which is perfect for that which is useless. What could be more useless than a cistern that holds no water?

I have noticed that I am tempted to lean on my own understanding when it comes to

- Disciplining or training a child with a behaviour that baffles me
- Picking out a homeschooling curriculum
- Wishing my husband would or would not make particular decision
- Dealing with issues of budget and finance
- Trying to respond to other people who are making life difficult for me

In these situations, I need to lean on God's understanding. I need to pray and search the scriptures for answers before deciding on a plan of action. I need to be able to say that "I walk by faith, not by sight" (2 Corinthians 5:7).

For further study:

Jeremiah 17, 7, 8 "Blessed is the man who trusts in the Lord, and whose hope is the Lord. For he shall be like a tree planted by the waters, which spreads out its roots by the river, and will not fear when heat comes, but its leaf will be green, and will not be anxious in the year of drought, nor will cease from yielding fruit."

Proverbs 28:26 "He who trusts in his own heart is a fool, but whoever walks wisely will be delivered."

Isaiah 47:10, 11 "For you have trusted in your wickedness; you have said, 'No one sees me.'" Your wisdom and your knowledge have warped you; and you have said in your heart, 'I am, and there is no one else besides me.' Therefore evil shall come upon you; you shall not know from where it arises. And trouble shall fall upon you; you will not be able to put it off. And desolation shall come upon you suddenly, which you shall not know."

Psalm 86:11 "Teach me Your way, O Lord; I will walk in Your truth; unite my heart to fear Your name."

16

A tale bearer reveals secrets, but he who is of a faithful spirit conceals a matter.
Proverbs 11:13

This verse has three applications for us. The first is that we are to be of a faithful spirit, and not a tale bearer who shares other people's secrets. When someone tells you something in confidence, keep that confidence. Even if it's not technically a secret, don't repeat what you heard. This includes what we share over the dinner table when our children are listening. "Conceals a matter" means that you don't even hint at the secret, letting others know that you know something. (There is the exception where a law is being broken and you must be faithful to God by reporting serious wrongdoing to the authorities, but this would be a very rare case).

The second application of this verse is that we need to be careful who we tell things too. Many times tale bearers are easy people to talk to; they have what an earlier generation would call "winning ways" about them, and we can easily be led into telling them what they want to know. If there is something that you don't want the general public to know, then entrust it to someone who is firm and true, mature in faith, and not a gossip.

The third application is that we need to avoid the society of tale bearers. If you are around one, you will hear the secrets of others. If we want to be faithful spirits who conceal matters, then we cannot be a party to gossip. It can be tempting for those of us who like knowing what is going on with other people, and those who like a good story, to tolerate the society of a tattler. As I said before, they are often very genial company. Often we homeschooling mothers are a bit lonely for female companionship, and we welcome the chance to have a good talk with another adult. But it is too high a price to pay for companionship if you are a willing party to such a sin. If you are in the company of a chatterbox who is sharing things she ought not to share, you should kindly and gently put a stop to the conversation. If it happens often, don't spend time with this woman.

A faithful spirit will guard both her mouth and her ears so that Christ is honoured in her conversations.

For further study:

I Corinthians 15:33 "Do not be deceived: 'Evil company corrupts good habits.'"

Psalm 5:9 "For there is no faithfulness in their mouth; their inward part is destruction; their throat is an open tomb; they flatter with their tongue."

Leviticus 19:16 "You shall not go about as a talebearer among your people; nor shall you take a stand against the life of your neighbour: I am the Lord."

I Timothy 5:13 "And besides they learn to be idle, wandering about from house to house, and not only idle but also gossips and busybodies, saying things which they ought not."

As a ring of gold in a swine's snout, so is a lovely woman who lacks discretion.
Proverbs 11:22

Rings through the nose were a common ornament at this time in Israel's history. They were considered an emblem of a wife's beauty. Contrast that with the image of a pig.

My husband once worked on a pig farm. The work was dirty and very, very smelly. (You can smell a pig farm a long time before you get to it!). He said the smell would cling to the workers, even after they had changed clothes and bathed. Piglets are cute, and I love little pig figurines that sit on a shelf, but a real pig living in my house would be very unpleasant.

Attaching a token of beauty like a ring to a pig—which is associated with uncleanness and rudeness—would be a demonstration of an oxymoron. Those two things are antithetical. If you are a beautiful woman but have no discretion, you will also be a walking oxymoron, and your beauty will not be attractive. So what is discretion?

It includes the idea of tactfulness, of sound judgement, and of a sense of what is fitting. It includes modesty in clothing, because a woman with discretion is aware of what is appropriate to wear. It includes how she assesses and responds to different theories and views. It also includes tone of voice and mode of speech, because that also involves awareness of what is fitting for the occasion. For example, if you've ever seen a beautiful woman suddenly use vulgar words or obscenities—and your admiration turns to disgust—you know what this verse is talking about!

Is there a place in your life where you lack discretion? Do you take as truth every idea with a certain label on it, or do you really search the Scriptures for guidance? Are your clothes appropriate to a woman who fears the Lord, or are your clothing choices guided more by a wish to appear young and trendy? Are you tactful in your words, and aware of your surroundings when you speak? (In other words, are you likely to be characterized as a "loudmouth"?) Many times we are unable to see where our problems are because we have gotten into habits that we never bother to assess.

Ask the Lord to show you where you should be more discreet. Ask your husband, too. He wants a wife that is beautiful on the inside as well as outwardly!

I Peter 3:3, 4 "Do not let your adornment be merely outward — arranging the hair, wearing gold, or putting on fine apparel — rather let it be the hidden person of the heart, with the incorruptible beauty of a gentle and quiet spirit, which is very precious in the sight of God.

Titus 2:3-5 "The older women likewise, that they be reverent in behavior, not slanderers, not given to much wine, teachers of good things — that they admonish the young women to love their husbands, to love their children, to be discreet, chaste, homemakers, good, obedient to their own husbands, that the word of God may not be blasphemed."

I Timothy 2:9-10 "In like manner also, that the women adorn themselves in modest apparel, with propriety and moderation, not with braided hair or gold or pearls or costly clothing, but, which is proper for women professing godliness, with good works."

Proverbs 9:13 "A foolish woman is clamorous; she is simple, and knows nothing."

18

He who spares his rod hates his son, but he who loves him disciplines him diligently.
Proverbs 13:24

I know many parents who hate their children, according to this verse. The parents themselves would protest about how much they love their children, and I have no doubt that they do have a lot of affection for their children, most of the time. But these parents do not discipline their children diligently.

They do discipline them sometimes — when the children are really getting on their nerves, or when they have done something too big to be overlooked, or when they are in a mood to "crack down" on bad behaviours. These parents will sometimes admit that they are not all that consistent in their disciplinary efforts. "But," they often add, "we're taking a balanced approach to parenting." These parents need to wrestle with this verse and others like it.

The reason this verse says that sparing your rod means hating your son is because the thing which usually gets in the way of diligent discipline is selfishness. To discipline diligently means that our efforts at discipline are not dependent on our mood that day, or on how busy we are at the moment, or if our sentimental affection gets the better of us ("Oh, he's just so precious, I can't bear to discipline him."). Is it loving to chastise a child one day for a certain offence, and let it go another day? At the very best, it keeps the child always pushing the boundaries to see what they can get away with. As they say here in Ireland, children are "chancers": they will always be willing to take the chance that this will be one of the times you won't discipline them. You will have a difficult time eliminating a bad behaviour if the child thinks he might get away with it. If you love your child, you will want to train his character in a godly way, and sparing the rod is not the way to do that. More seriously, it will be hard for a child to understand how God's laws are always enforced by God, when their main authority figures don't always enforce the rules they set.

So what is the answer? See to it that you love your child. Make sure discipline is done in a spirit of love and not anger. Examine your heart to see that you are chastising because you truly want to train your child in righteousness, and not because you feel that retribution is necessary. Once you set the rules, stick to them. Stick to them even when you're feeling lazy or indulgent. Try to forget about your own inconveniences and difficulties, and ask God to put true love in your heart for your child.

For further study:

Proverbs 23:13, 14 "Do not withhold correction from a child, for if you beat him with a rod, he will not die. You shall beat him with a rod, and deliver his soul from hell."

Proverbs 22:6 "Train up a child in the way he should go, and when he is old he will not depart from it."
Ephesians 6:4 "And you, fathers, do not provoke your children to wrath, but bring them up in the training and admonition of the Lord."

19

He who is slow to wrath has great understanding, but he who is impulsive exalts folly. Proverbs 14:29

Are you easily frustrated? How much does it take to make you angry? If we want to be wise women, we need to have a "long fuse." You may know that being easily angered is a sin, but were you aware how much the Bible links it with foolishness? Proverbs 14:17 says that "A quick tempered man acts foolishly" and Ecclesiastes 7:9 warns, "Do not hasten in your spirit to be angry, for anger rests in the bosom of fools."

Why is it foolish to be quick tempered? Well, for one thing, a quick temper is a sin that is always accompanied by others. Our anger usually shows itself in unedifying words or violent actions. It usually causes strife ("An angry man stirs up strife, and a furious man abounds in transgression." Proverbs 29:22). And if we are angry at our children, then we are provoking them to anger, which God expressly forbids (Ephesians 6:4).

We can easily see the foolishness of anger when it is demonstrated in a toddler. Have you seen the exhibition some toddlers put on when they don't get their way? They are so ridiculous it can be hard to keep from laughing at them. Grown-ups are just as ridiculous when they are angry — the more angry you are, the less rational you are — but it is not as funny because an adult has the capacity to do so much more harm than a toddler.

If we want to stop losing our tempers, we must begin before there is anything to provoke us. We need to put on the virtue of patience, as well as putting off the sin of anger. Here are some ideas that may help in developing a patient spirit:

- Meditate on the character of God. Nahum 1:3 says that "The Lord is slow to anger."
- Memorize Scripture that deals directly with being long-suffering and patient, and think about them often.
- Think through what tends to trigger angry emotions in you, and pray about what you can do to deal with these things in a godly way.
- Pray fervently and consistently for victory in this area of your life. Don't become discouraged and give up if you feel like you just keep failing in this. Just confess your sin to God and to those you sinned against, and keep going.

Anger can destroy our families; praise God that we have the resources and power (through Christ) to overcome it!

For further study:

Psalm 37:8 "Cease from anger, and forsake wrath; do not fret—it only causes harm."

Proverbs 16:32 "He who is slow to anger is better than the mighty, and he who rules his spirit than he who takes a city."

Proverbs 21:19 "Better to dwell in the wilderness, than with a contentious and angry woman."

20

Keep your heart with all diligence, for out of it spring the issues of life. Proverbs 4:23

In the Hebrew way of thinking, the word "heart" meant not the physical organ, but the whole inner man: the mind, emotions and will. Keep watch over your heart and make sure it stays centered on the Word of God. We are to do this, it says, because out of our hearts spring the issues of life—our behaviour, words, and attitudes. Jesus alluded to this fact when he said, "For from within, out of the heart of men, proceed evil thoughts, adulteries, fornications, murders, thefts, covetousness, wickedness, deceit, lewdness, an evil eye, blasphemy, pride, foolishness. All these evil things come from within and defile a man." (Mark 7:21-23)

So how do we keep watch over our hearts? The first thing to do is to saturate our minds with Scripture. Our goal should be to know Scripture so well that the moment we hear a wrong statement or even think a wrong thought, a little voice in our minds would be saying, "That's not true; remember this Bible verse that says the opposite?" The best defence of our hearts is to have God's Word hidden in them.

Secondly, we need to examine what we are exposing ourselves to. Whatever goes into your mind will stay there, and have some influence on you. Some things are not evil in themselves, but can be unhealthy for some ladies, especially if there is more than just occasional exposure. I have heard many ladies say they have decided to cut out Christian fiction—especially the romance ones, because those books were starting to make them discontent with their own husbands. Many families have done away with the television completely, saying that the tiny bit of profit there may be in some shows wasn't worth wading through the rest of the stuff for (commercials included!). One lady stopped subscribing to a decorating magazine, because it was feeding her discontentment with her home. I personally don't mind reading a classic novel now and again, but a steady diet of them (stories told from a non-Christian point of view) is bad for my heart.

Thirdly, be aware of what your mind dwells on. Daydreaming is a habit that many women fall into. Sometimes they are the heroines of whatever story they are making up in their heads, which feeds their pride. Sometimes they are daydreaming about their husbands acting the way they wish they would act, which feeds their discontentment with the way things actually are. Sometimes they dream about men other than their husbands being romantic towards them, and this (not surprisingly) can lead to adultery.

Whether we are pleasing to God or not ultimately depends on the state of our hearts. No wonder God's Word admonishes us to keep watch over our hearts!

For further study:

Matthew 26:41 "Watch and pray, lest you enter into temptation. The spirit indeed is willing, but the flesh is weak."

I Peter 5:8 "Be sober, be vigilant; because your adversary the devil walks about like a roaring lion, seeking whom he may devour."

I Peter 1:13 "Therefore, gird up the loins of your mind, be sober, and rest your hope fully upon the grace that is to be brought to you at the revelation of Jesus Christ."

21

The lazy man does not roast what he took in hunting, but diligence is man's precious possession. Proverbs 12:27

This verse describes a lazy hunter who does part of the work necessary (he hunts the food) but then he doesn't finish the job (cooking it) and the food is wasted. "How silly," we might think. "If I went to all the work of hunting an animal, surely I would roast it so I could eat it!" But we've probably all done something similar.

I know women who have books, tapes, and videos galore on managing their time and their homes, being a godly wife, and parenting in a biblical way. And yet they've never taken steps to implement all this wisdom. We can make an investment of time and money to learn how to better fulfil our God-given responsibilities, and yet if we do not put it into practice, it becomes food we have hunted for, but have not prepared. What a waste! What good is all of that wisdom sitting on a shelf or swirling around in your head, if it makes no difference to the way you live?

The fact that we have procured this information in one way or another means that we are interested in doing what God wants us to. But like the hunter in this verse, we are lazy. We feel a sense of satisfaction, perhaps, at having gotten all these resources, and think that we are therefore on the way to being what we should be. And certainly, knowledge is the first step. But until we start to act on it, it will remain a waste of time and money. James 1:22 says, "But be doers of the word, and not hearers only, deceiving yourselves." We can hear what we ought to do over and over again, but if it stops with hearing, we are deceiving ourselves.

The key to overcoming this problem is diligence, as the verse points out. What a truly precious thing diligence is!

For further study:

Ecclesiastes 9:10 "Whatever your hand finds to do, do it with your might; for there is no work or device or knowledge or wisdom in the grave where you are going."

Psalm 119:60 "I made haste, and did not delay to keep Your commandments."

22

Let your eyes look straight ahead, and your eyelids look right before you. Ponder the path of your feet, and let all your ways be established. Do not turn to the right or the left; remove your foot from evil. Proverbs 4:25-27

These verses talk about being steadfast in the path of wisdom, and not being distracted. Do you know what God has called you to do? Then do it, and don't let yourself veer off that path. It is easy for us to be swayed by moods, circumstances, or pressure from other people, and therefore God wants us to learn to have our eyes looking directly ahead, and our gaze fixed in front of us.

This is not a call to stubbornness, however. When verse 26 says, "ponder the path of your feet," it means to consider carefully the way you are going. Suppose your family has a particular conviction about an area of life that is not shared by many (or most) Christian families. If you begin to have doubts about this particular conviction, you should "ponder the path of your feet," and consider it in the light of Scripture, pray about it, and perhaps ask counsel. You may end up changing your minds about it. But if you come away from doing those things still convinced that this is the right course for your family, then you should humbly continue to walk that path. By contrast, Proverbs 5:6 describes the immoral woman as one whose "ways are unstable; you do not know them."

Of course, these verses are also talking about keeping away from actual sin. Is there a particular sin you are struggling with today? A bitter thought, an exasperated tone of voice, a lack of self control, a lie that would get you out of a sticky situation? If so, keep your feet on the path of righteousness! Remember the blessings that come with a life of obedience, and think of the detrimental effects your sin has not only on yourself, but also on your whole family. It's not worth it! In Jeremiah 5:25, God tells His wicked people, "Your iniquities have turned these things away, and your sins have withheld good from you." Our sin has consequences; one of the consequences is that it may keep us from having the good things that God wants His children to enjoy.

For further reading:

Isaiah 30:21 "Your ears shall hear a word behind you, saying, 'This is the way, walk in it,' whenever you turn to the right hand or whenever you turn to the left."

I Corinthians 15:58 "Therefore, my beloved brethren, be steadfast, immovable, always abounding in the work of the Lord, knowing that your labor is not in vain in the Lord."

23

There is one who speaks like the piercings of a sword, but the tongue of the wise promotes health. Proverbs 12:18

The Hebrew word for "speaks" in this verse means "to speak out," and often has the connotation of speaking recklessly and without thought (*Proverbs, Ecclesiastes, Song of Songs, Commentary on the Old Testament*, Keil and Delitzsch, Hedrickson Publishers, Inc., 1966, p.189). Our reckless words can do great damage and cause a lot of hurt, just like a sword.

Many times in my life, I have hurt people unintentionally with my words. At least two of those times, I was trying to be funny. I was trying to appear clever and witty, and so I didn't think through the impact of my words before I said them. Both times, there were repercussions for months! Another time, I assumed another person felt a certain way, and viewed her own actions in a particular light. I stated this as if it was an obvious fact, and went on to give my own assessment of things. Weeks later, this person told me how hurt she was, because I had misread her intentions and not even asked her what she was actually thinking.

As badly as I feel over these incidents, I feel worse over the careless words I have spoken to my own family. Words that seemed to belittle my husband, words that drained the joy out of my children's accomplishments. So much damage can be done without our even being aware of it! It might make us want to not talk at all to avoid injuring others as if we were a piercing sword! But the last half of the verse gives us motivation to use wise words. "Promotes health" could also be translated "brings healing." When someone is hurting, wise words will soften the hurt. God can use us to encourage others, and bind up the wounds of their hearts.

But where do we get wise words? How do we know what to say? The world's wisdom will do no lasting good. The secular talk shows that feature popular psychology intended to make people feel good about themselves give no real help to hurting people. But we know that God's Word has all the answers for our problems. If our minds are filled with Scripture, then truth and words of blessing will be on our lips.

For further study:

Proverbs 29:20 "Do you see a man hasty in his words? There is more hope for a fool than for him."

Colossians 4:6 "Let your speech always be with grace, seasoned with salt, that you may know how you ought to answer each one."

24

The king's heart is in the hand of the Lord, like the rivers of water; He turns it wherever He wishes. Proverbs 21:1

This is one of the most comforting verses in the Bible. It shows us that God is in control of the authorities in our lives, and that He directs their actions. That should be such a relief for us!

Many Christian women, especially those who have read books, gone to seminars, and listened to tapes about having a Christian home, have a very definite idea about the way they want their husbands to be. They have a spiritual standard in their minds that he doesn't match up to, and they feel compelled to nag, "hint," complain, or lecture him into meeting that standard. The good news of this verse is that God can accomplish what He wants to in our husbands' hearts without us doing anything! That isn't to say that we shouldn't do all we can to encourage our husbands in right ways as they seek to obey God, but it does mean that we will not be trying to manipulate the circumstances.

Another application of this verse has to do with submission. For all of us women who are married, the human authority that has the most influence over our lives is our husbands. God tells us very clearly that wives are supposed to submit to their husbands (Ephesians 5:22-24). But the Bible also tells us why wives often don't want to submit. I Peter 3 1-6 says again that wives need to submit to their husbands, and gives the example of Sarah obeying Abraham as a model to follow. Then it says, "whose daughters you are if you do good and are not afraid with any terror." In other words, we are tempted not to submit because we are afraid of the consequences if we do.

This verse is comforting because it reminds us that the decisions our husbands make are within the sovereignty of God, and nothing will happen to us that is outside of God's will for our lives. So we can do as the Bible says and submit to our husbands as to the Lord with the confidence that God will take care of the results. He is in control!

For further study:

Ephesians 5:22-24 "Wives, submit to your own husbands, as to the Lord. For the husband is head of the wife, as also Christ is head of the church; and He is the

Savior of the body. Therefore, just as the church is subject to Christ, so let the wives be to their own husbands in everything."

I Peter 3:1-6 "Wives, likewise, be submissive to your own husbands, that even if some do not obey the word, they, without a word, may be won by the conduct of their wives, when they observe your chaste conduct accompanied by fear. Do not let your adornment be merely outward—arranging the hair, wearing gold, or putting on fine apparel—rather let it be the hidden person of the heart, with the incorruptible beauty of a gentle and quiet spirit, which is very precious in the sight of God. For in this manner, in former times, the holy women who trusted in God also adorned themselves, being submissive to their own husbands, as Sarah obeyed Abraham, calling him lord, whose daughters you are if you do good and are not afraid with any terror.

Romans 8:28 "And we know that all things work together for good to those who love God, to those who are the called according to His purpose."

25

The wise woman builds her house, but the foolish pulls it down with her hands.
Proverbs 14:1

What does it mean to build your house? It means to keep the household running well, keeping the physical things in order as well as keeping the family relationships harmonious and strong. There are so many elements to building up a house, and pages and pages could be written about each one. Before I make a little list for you to think through, let me remind you that you cannot work on every single area at once! But you can concentrate on one thing at a time without being overwhelmed, and you will be building your house all the while.

The wise woman who wants to build her house will pay attention to the following areas:

• Relationships — husband-wife, parent-child, child-child — are they honouring to God?

• Child training — are the children growing in the biblical virtues and learning to contribute to the running of the household?

• Attitudes — is there an atmosphere of cheerfulness and love evident in the home?

• The physical home — is it relatively clean and tidy, and are things well taken care of?

• Routines — are things done haphazardly or on schedule and with a purpose?

• Finances — is the part for which we are responsible in good order?

In whichever area you are weakest, find resources to help you! Read books, ask counsel of a woman who is strong in that area, and ask your husband for suggestions. Purpose to work on one issue until it is no longer a problem, and then work on something else. The foolish woman tears down her house with her own hands. Often she does this through neglect. By not actively working to build your house, you are contributing to its destruction.

Almost without exception, the mother sets the tone for the home. If she neglects her duties and tears down her house, the father can do very little to stop the destruction of his home. We do have a great responsibility, sisters, but what an incredible privilege it is as well! God is able to make us wise women who can not only carry this burden but do it with ease! Do you believe He is able to do that for *you*? He is!! Start today to build your home for your own benefit, as well as your family's.

For further study:

Titus 2:4, 5 "That they admonish the young women to love their husbands, to love their children, to be discreet, chaste, homemakers, good, obedient to their own husbands, that the word of God may not be blasphemed."

Proverbs 31:27 "She watches over the ways of her household, and does not eat the bread of idleness."

Proverbs 7:11 "She was loud and rebellious, her feet would not stay at home."

26

Do not withhold good from those to whom it is due, when it is in the power of your hand to do so. Proverbs 3:27

Have you ever done the following?

- Put off getting food prepared even though everyone was hungry, because you were too engrossed in what you were doing at the moment?
- Neglected to pay a bill—perhaps a library fine—because money is a bit tight this month?
- Didn't prepare homeschooling lessons because you were feeling lazy at the time you should have been preparing?
- Let days go by without praying for your husband and others who need your prayers?

I have done all of those things, and many more as well. The root cause is simply selfishness. Sometimes I don't "feel" like doing what I should be doing, and I allow the world's philosophies to justify my selfishness. The world says, "Take time for yourself; don't overdo it; relax without feeling guilty; don't worry about it." But God says that we should not put off doing good when it is in our power to do it.

I am not saying that we should never rest, never take a break, or never do anything we enjoy. I am also not saying that when a child requests something we need to drop what we're doing, jump up, and run to cater to their desire. Sometimes they need to learn to wait patiently! But there is a vast difference between asking a child to wait for the purpose of their character development and making them wait because it's not what we feel like doing at the moment. I have noticed that when I am engrossed in a book, I am very likely to put off doing the good that I should be doing. This means that I need to keep myself from getting engrossed in a book until my duties are done.

Some women, while they are not lazy, do pursue their own agendas and end up withholding good from others because they are too focused on their own goals to take others' needs into consideration. An example might be a mother whose goal for the day is to organize the closets, and she does so by neglecting almost everything not related to her goal, including cuddling the little ones and showing deference to her husband's goals and wishes.

Let us learn to be selfless, and look for opportunities of doing good rather than withholding it.

For further study:

Titus 3:14 "And let our people also lean to maintain good words, to meet urgent needs, that they may not be unfruitful."

2 Corinthians 9:8 "And God is able to make all grace abound toward you, that you, always having all sufficiency in all things, may have an abundance for every good work."

2 Thessalonians 3:13 "But as for you, brethren, do not grow weary in doing good."

27

A fool vents all his feelings, but a wise man holds them back. Proverbs 29:11

Have you ever said, "I've had such a bad day and I just need to vent!"? We can mean a couple of things by that. One thing might be, "I have all these thoughts and feelings that I'd like to express to someone so that I can untangle them and start thinking biblically about them." If that is what we mean, then that is fine—assuming we are talking to an appropriate person at an appropriate time! But sometimes we mean, "I'm just going to do a little complaining here, but I'm going to call it venting because it doesn't sound sinful that way."

Most women have an innate desire to share whatever they're feeling. They feel alone and lonely when there's no one they can share their emotions with. God has made us to be emotional creatures, and to want to communicate that with others. So far, so good. But just because we have the desire to share doesn't mean we always need to do it! Foolishness comes in when, as this verse says, we vent all our feelings without discretion. Here are some examples of times when a wise woman will keep her mouth shut:

- Any time she feels like complaining.
- Any time she is angry. If there is sin on the part of another person, a biblical rebuke may be in order, but only after she is calm and has forgiven them in her heart.
- When she feels her husband needs a loving reproof, but she has not taken time to consider her words and pray over it.
- When the person she is talking to is under stress, and her words will only add to the burden.

The root sin behind all this is a lack of self-control. As we grow in self-control in other areas of life, we will find more victory in this issue as well. James 3:2 says, "For we all stumble in many things. If anyone does not stumble in word, he is a perfect [or mature] man, able also to bridle the whole body." Another thing that will help is to be in the habit of constantly conversing with God. He already knows all our feelings, and can guide us through appropriate responses to them. Ask Him to help you, and He will.

For further study:

Proverbs 29:20 "Do you see a man hasty in his words? There is more hope for a fool than for him."

Proverbs 10:19 "In the multitude of words sin is not lacking, but he who restrains his lips is wise."

Job 13:5 "Oh, that you would be silent, and it would be your wisdom!"

Psalm 141:3 "Set a guard, O Lord, over my mouth; keep watch over the door of my lips."

28

If you faint in the day of adversity, your strength is small. Proverbs 24:10

How much does it take for you to faint? That is the question I had to ask myself today. I had had great plans for myself today. The children were going to learn some new chores, the schedule was going to go well, and I had some new ideas to use in dealing with certain character issues in the children. But two of the children were ill in the night, and my sleep was broken many times. I was tired when I got up, and even though the children were not very sick when they woke up, I decided it was too much work to even do the schedule today. This evening as I pondered over what I hadn't accomplished today, it struck me that this is really a pattern in my life. I may have great plans and ideas and even be full of enthusiasm for them, but if I don't feel well or am tired, or any other difficulty presents itself, then the plan is laid aside.

I am reminded of Paul's admonition to Timothy, to "be ready in season and out of season" (I Tim. 4:2). God cannot greatly use a man in ministry unless that man can be depended on to do his ministry whether it is convenient or not, popular or not, easy or not. If you were choosing someone to train a group of elite soldiers who had an important task to do, would you choose someone who didn't show up to work whenever he had a cold, or one who let the soldiers off training if he didn't feel like putting them through their workouts? Hardly! You'd pick someone who was there and working hard unless it was physically impossible to so.

In the same way, if we give up whenever the way looks difficult, or it is inconvenient, or we are tired, or have a headache, then our strength is small. Mother-work is wonderful work. It has huge potential for impacting the world with the gospel, as we raise up soldiers of the cross. Wouldn't you love it if God could say of you, "That woman is dependable. She doesn't do as I ask her just when it suits her and when it is easy. She does it even when she doesn't feel like it, and works as well and as wisely as it is possible for her to work."

Are you a woman that God sees as dependable? Or is your strength small, so that you are unable to keep going in the right way when it is not convenient? May God make us mighty women that He can use for His kingdom!

Isaiah 40:29 "He gives power to the weak, and to those who have no might He increases strength."

I Corinthians 15:58 "Therefore, my beloved brethren, be steadfast, immovable, always abounding in the work of the Lord, knowing that your labor is not in vain in the Lord."

Galatians 6:9 "And let us not grow weary while doing good, for in due season we shall reap if we do not lose heart."

29

The silver-haired head is a crown of glory, if it is found in the way of righteousness.
Proverbs 16:31

In the last year, I have found more and more grey hairs on my head. I have dark brown hair, so they stand out! I wish I could say that I was excited about getting them, but I wasn't. I didn't want to feel old, I wanted to stay young…or at least look young! When I turned thirty a couple years ago, it was a little bit difficult for me. I tried to comfort myself with statements like, "Well, thirty isn't so old. Most people would still call you a young woman!" But even as I said it I was aware that that was a foolish thing to take comfort in. It won't be many years before that won't be true and I will have to face up to the fact that *I am no longer young*! So I made it a matter of prayer and study, and this is what I learned.

I discovered that I was bothered by getting older because I had bought into the world's lie that life is better for the young. I wanted to be the beautiful young woman who is the heroine in most love stories (ok, I've never been all that beautiful, but I was young, at least!). When I was in my twenties and achieved something people found noteworthy, they often said, "And you're so young to have done that, too!" I liked that admiration. I was idolizing what the world worships.

Once I repented of my wrong desires, I found some things that did comfort me. One was the realization that God wants me to be the exact age I am now. I can submit to His will, or I can rebel (however fruitlessly) against it. There are enough warnings in Scripture about rebelling against God that I decided on the former option! Another comfort is that this verse is telling the truth: to be an older person who is found in the way of righteousness is a very desirable thing. If I am faithful to my God, if I grow in the wisdom and knowledge of God, and if I know *Him* all my life, think how close I will be to the Lord when I am aged! Isn't that something to look forward to?

For further study:

Proverbs 20:29 "The glory of young men is their strength, and the splendour off old men is their grey head."

Isaiah 46:4 "Even to your old age, I am He, and even to grey hairs I will carry you! I have made, and I will bear; even I will carry, and will deliver you."

30

He who is devoid of wisdom despises his neighbour, but a man of understanding holds his peace. Proverbs 11:12

According to the great Hebrew scholar Delitzsch, this verse refers to someone who degrades his neighbour in a derisive or insulting manner, whether publicly or privately. (*Proverbs, Ecclesiastes, Song of Songs, Commentary on the Old Testament,* Keil and Delitzsch, Hedrickson Publishers, Inc., 1966, page 171.)

Church "cry rooms," nurseries, homeschooling support group meetings, baby showers, wedding showers....whenever women get together, there is a danger that someone will deride their neighbour. Whatever our particular convictions and methods are, it is very easy for us to criticize our neighbours who don't share those convictions and methods, or who have some that we think are silly.

"How could she just let her baby cry like that? In our house, anyone can eat when they're hungry!"

"Doesn't she know that feeding on a schedule is so much better than demand feeding?"

"Of course, they don't really care about the welfare of their children—they send them to public school!"

"They never allow their children around any unbelievers...how are those kids going to learn to evangelize?"

"I don't know why they allow their children to play sports; the influence of the other children will drag them down."

"Those kids eat so much sugar! I would never let my kids eat that kind of junk!"

Sometimes we even make comments to people's faces in a way that puts them down. The Bible says that when we do this, we are lacking judgement. I may think that the other person is acting like a fool, but this verse tells me that I am the fool if I talk this way.

The remedy, according to this verse, is to learn to be silent. Few and far between are the issues that really need to be talked about. Most of the things we feel so strongly about are really preference issues, and we need to back off and keep quiet. If a woman really is in unrepentant sin, then you need to talk to her in love and try to restore her relationship with God. If she refuses to listen to you, then you need to follow the steps outlined in Matthew 18. But on no account do you need to talk to any other women about it! If a woman does ask you for your opinion or advice, you may give it, but do it in such a way that it would give offence to no one. Remember: "Let all that you do be done in love" (I Corinthians 16:14).

For further study:

I Corinthians 13:1-8a "Though I speak with the tongues of men and of angels, but have not love, I have become sounding brass or a clanging cymbal. And though I have the gift of prophecy, and understand all mysteries and all knowledge, and though I have all faith, so that I could remove mountains, but have not love, I am nothing. And though I bestow all my goods to feed the poor, and though I give my body to be burned, but have not love, it profits me nothing. Love suffers long and is kind; love does not envy; love does not parade itself, is not puffed up; does not behave rudely, does not seek its own, is not provoked, thinks no evil; does not rejoice in iniquity, but rejoices in the truth; bears all things, believes all things, hopes all things, endures all things. Love never fails."

Ephesians 4:29 "Let no corrupt word proceed out of your mouth, but what is good for necessary edification, that it may impart grace to the hearers."

Colossians 4:6 "Let your speech always be with grace, seasoned with salt, that you may know how you ought to answer each one."

31

He who walks with wise men will be wise, but the companion of fools will be destroyed.
Proverbs 13:20

This verse speaks about the influence our companions have over us. How would you characterize your friends? Are they wise women or are they foolish? When you spend time with them, are you pulled down in your walk with God, or are you encouraged all the more to keep walking with the Lord?

You may not think this verse applies to you because you don't have women that you regularly spend time with. Many homeschooling moms are too busy with their homes and families to have time to "hang out" with friends. Or perhaps you have in the past decided that the women you were spending time with were more foolish than wise, and you decided not to be close friends with them anymore. You might even be in a position to say that you have no close friends at all. Can you then skip this verse?

No. Your companions don't need to be with you in the flesh to be an influence on you. You can be influenced by non-present companions in books, magazines, videos, television, email loops, and internet chat rooms. It is the amount of time that you spend being exposed to the ideas and advice of someone else that makes them a "companion." There are two ways that a foolish companion (physically present or not) can influence you.

1. *A world view that is unbiblical.* This was brought home to me when I was studying for a major exam in literature. I was required to read dozens of books, poems and essays and to be able to discuss them at great length. Well, I knew there were some pieces of literature that I just couldn't read as a Christian, so I didn't, and trusted God for the result of the exam. The ones that I did choose to read really had nothing bad in them. But I read them all in a short space of time, which meant that for several weeks my mind was occupied for large amounts of time in seeing the world and life's events through the eyes of someone who wasn't seeing properly (because they weren't looking at life from a biblical perspective). It was a drag to my spiritual life. If you are constantly exposed to a view of the world that isn't biblical, it will drag you down—if only because you will have to expend so much mental energy combating the false philosophies you are confronted with.

2. *Unbiblical advice.* Psalm 1:1 describes the blessed man as one who "walks not in the counsel of the ungodly." If you need advice about your life, make sure the one who is advising you is wise, and using the Scripture to counsel you.

For further study:

Psalm 1:1 "Blessed is the man who walks not in the counsel of the ungodly, nor stands in the path of sinners, nor sits in the seat of the scornful."

Proverbs 12:26 "The righteous should choose his friends carefully, for the way of the wicked leads them astray."

Proverbs 14:7 "Go from the presence of a foolish man, when you do not perceive in him the lips of knowledge."

32

A generous man will prosper; he who refreshes others will himself be refreshed.
Proverbs 11:25

For homeschooling mothers, there is always a danger that we will spread ourselves too thin. Many moms have discovered that in order to give proper attention to managing their households, they have needed to cut back on commitments outside the home. This is a good thing; if your primary responsibilities are not being fulfilled well, it is not pleasing to God to be using your time to do other things. And certainly the main ministry of a wife and mother is her own family.

However, we can be tempted to use this as an excuse not to minister at all. We feel overworked, tired, and listless; we begin to just "go through the motions." In this state, how could we have enough energy to help anyone else? Perhaps we feel this way because we have *not* been ministering to others. After all, "he who refreshes others will himself be refreshed."

If we need to decline the official avenues of ministry that our church offers, then we need to be creative in finding other ways that we can serve others. Teaching Sunday School, attending a ladies Bible study, or running Vacation Bible School are not the only ways you can serve (although there is certainly nothing wrong with doing these if you can!).

Here are some things you might consider as a way to refresh others:

- Spend time praying just for the needs of those outside your family
- Make meals to take to families whose mothers are ill or recovering from childbirth (one night make a double portion of dinner and freeze the extra, and then it will be ready immediately when a need comes up).
- Send encouraging notes, emails, or care packages to missionary families — I can assure you that this definitely refreshes them!
- Find ways as a family to be involved in an evangelistic outreach. For example, go twice a month to a nursing home and talk to the residents there (getting permission first, of course).
- Give money to the church or to a family that needs it. After all, the first part of the verse says, "A generous man will prosper."
- Offer to watch the children of another family for free one evening, so the parents can have time alone.

- Have international students or other lonely people to your house for meals.

Whatever you decide, plan to do it and mark it on your calendar, otherwise it won't get done! And once you've done it, if your ministry was done from the heart and for the purpose of glorifying God, you will indeed be refreshed.

For further study:

I Peter 4:9, 10 "Be hospitable to one another without grumbling. As each one has received a gift, minister it to one another, as good stewards of the manifold grace of God."

2 Corinthians 9:7, 8 "So let each one give as he purposes in his heart, not grudgingly or of necessity; for God loves a cheerful giver. And God is able to make all grace abound toward you, that you, always having all sufficiency in all things, may have an abundance for every good work."

Romans 12:13 "distributing to the needs of the saints, given to hospitality."

Galatians 6:10 "Therefore, as we have opportunity, let us do good to all, especially to those who are of the household of faith."

33

Whoever loves discipline loves knowledge, but he who hates correction is stupid.
Proverbs 12:1

One way that we can be disciplined and reproved is by God. Job 5:17 says, "Behold, happy is the man whom God corrects; Therefore do not despise the chastening of the Almighty." We can see from this verse that discipline from God is for our good, and something to welcome. It is not fun to be corrected by God; Hebrews 12:11 tells us that "no chastening seems to be joyful for the present, but painful; nevertheless, afterwards it yields the peaceable fruit of righteousness." God may chasten us by letting the natural consequences of sin take their toll on us, or by sending some particular difficulty our way. He also corrects us by using the Holy Spirit to convict us about our sin. If we respond to this and change our ways, He may not have to discipline us more harshly.

We can also be rebuked by other people. Psalm 141:5a says, "Let the righteous strike me; It shall be a kindness. And let him rebuke me: It shall be as excellent oil; Let my head not refuse it." We should welcome the reproof of other people, since it helps us to get rid of areas of sin in our lives and make us more like our Saviour.

But it's easy to hate correction, isn't it? Our pride is always hurt that someone sees an area of weakness big enough to rebuke us for. Our natural desire is to react with an excuse or an attack on the person who is trying to instruct us ("you're not so great yourself, you know.") Especially if the one rebuking is a member of our own family! Sometimes the reproof is not given in a loving way, and that makes it easier for us to brush it aside ("He's always complaining about the state of the house....I'd like to see *him* try to keep it clean with four small children and homeschooling! And he never does anything to help....")

If anyone has a criticism of you, try to see if there's any just cause for it. They may have exaggerated the magnitude of the problem, but if there is anything you can improve on, then be thankful for a chance to make yourself more pleasing to God in that area. It will prove that you love knowledge and are not stupid. And always remember: if anyone knew you as well as you know yourself, they would have a lot more to rebuke you for, wouldn't they? For every unjust criticism you may receive there are probably dozens that you deserve and won't get!

Hebrews 12:6-11 "For whom the Lord loves He chastens, and scourges every son whom He receives. If you endure chastening, God deals with you as with sons; for what son is there whom a father does not chasten? But if you are without chastening, of which all have become partakers, then you are illegitimate and not sons. Furthermore, we have had human fathers who corrected us, and we paid them respect. Shall we not much more readily be in subjection to the Father of spirits and live? For they indeed for a few days chastened us as seemed best to them, but He for our profit, that we may be partakers of His holiness. Now no chastening seems to be joyful for the present, but painful; nevertheless, afterward it yields the peaceable fruit of righteousness to those who have been trained by it."

Revelation 3:19 "As many as I love, I rebuke and chasten. Therefore be zealous and repent."

Proverbs 27:5 "Open rebuke is better than love carefully concealed."

Proverbs 29:1 "He who is often rebuked, and hardens his neck, will suddenly be destroyed, and that without remedy."

34

The mouth of the righteous brings forth wisdom, but the perverse tongue will be cut out. The lips of the righteous know what is acceptable, but the mouth of the wicked what is perverse. Proverbs 10:31, 32

In this verse we have a contrast between the speech of the righteous and that of the wicked. The first thing we learn about a righteous mouth is that it speaks wisdom. The book of James gives us a description of what wisdom is, and we could compare these characteristics to our speech: "But the wisdom that is from above is first pure, then peaceable, gentle, willing to yield, full of mercy and good fruits, without partiality, and without hypocrisy" (James 3:17). Would you say that your speech is characterized by wisdom as defined here? Or do you speak many unwise words?

The other thing mentioned about a righteous mouth is that it knows what is acceptable. The root word for "acceptable" can also mean "pleasing," probably here implying "pleasing to God." There is no mystery about what sort of speech is pleasing to God. We know that it is to be edifying, gracious, wholesome, sweet, and full of blessing (Ephesians 4:29, Colossians 4:6, Proverbs 16:21, James 3:10).

The wicked tongue is also described here, and labelled "perverse." Though this would include the idea of sexually perverted talk, it is not limited to that. It also means to be twisted away from what is right. Basically, any speech that deviates from what God wants it to be could be labelled perverse. The Bible tells us very clearly what things should not come out of our mouths. Lying, malice, filthy language, slander, flattery, violent talk, harsh words, foolishness, contention, and blasphemy are all clearly denounced, often in several different places (Colossians 3:8, Proverbs 10:6, 18, Proverbs 26:28, Proverbs 15:1,2). Are any of these things characteristic of your speech? Go over the list again, one by one, and see whether you have allowed yourself to speak any of these kind of words to your husband, your children, people in the church, extended family members, other acquaintances, strangers, or even to yourself! This kind of talk has no place in our lives!

This proverb warns us that there are grave consequences for careless speech: "the perverse tongue will be cut out." We are also reminded of what Jesus said about our words: "But I say to you that for every idle word men may speak, they will give account of it in the day of judgement" (Matthew 12:26). While this should, in one sense, scare us into good behaviour, we should also remember that God is anxious to help us with our mouth problems! He is not waiting to pounce on our first wicked word and condemn us for it; instead He delights in every pure word we speak. Ask Him to help you, and He will answer you.

For further study:

Colossians 3:8 "But now you yourselves are to put off all these: anger, wrath, malice, blasphemy, filthy language out of your mouth."

Proverbs 10:6, 18 "Blessings are on the head of the righteous, but violence covers the mouth of the wicked...Whoever hides hatred has lying lips, and whoever spreads slander is a fool."

Proverbs 26:28 "A lying tongue hates those who are crushed by it, and a flattering mouth works ruin."

Proverbs 15:1, 2 "A soft answer turns away wrath, but a harsh word stirs up anger. The tongue of the wise uses knowledge rightly, but the mouth of fools pours forth foolishness."

I Peter 2:1 "Therefore, laying aside all malice, all deceit, hypocrisy, envy, and all evil speaking..."

35

He who has a slack hand becomes poor, but the hand of the diligent makes rich.
Proverbs 10:4

This verse about diligence deals with money. One application of it would be to work hard at earning money; otherwise you will be poor. However, since most homeschooling mothers are not the breadwinners in their homes, we need to think about how this verse applies to us.

Often our husbands make us stewards of the money they earn. We are usually the ones buying groceries, household products, homeschooling materials, and clothes. Sometimes we are even the ones paying the monthly bills. Sometimes money is tight, and our husbands rely on our diligence in being frugal to make ends meet.

I'll never forget the lady who wrote in to an internet forum, saying that she really should cut down on her spending, but there were some things (like her cell phone) that she felt she really couldn't do without. A wise woman wrote back in reply: "Whenever we start with 'I want to ABC but can't because of XYZ...' then we are not being true to ourselves. Much better to say, 'I want to carry on living just as I am, I want this to all be done with, and I want all the things I already have.' I am familiar with the 'I want to BUT...' That one word will paralyse you. Instead, try 'I want to and therefore I WILL...'"

Diligence means self-discipline. If you don't want your family to be poor (or poorer!), then you must not have a slack hand in your financial transactions. Make a budget and stick to it! Don't tell yourself that you deserve a little treat after being good all week. If you don't have enough money to buy anything more this month, then don't go shopping, don't look at catalogues, and don't browse through online stores. Just as you tell your little ones "don't touch that" and expect them to obey, tell yourself "don't buy that" and walk—or run—away.

There may be ways you can contribute to the family purse as well: hold a garage sale, help your husband in his work, sell some things you make....you can be creative. Do make sure, however, that whatever you do you are not slighting the priorities that God has ordained for you.

May we contribute to and manage well our family's finances, and not impoverish them by our lack of diligence.

For further study:

Titus 2:12 "teaching us that, denying ungodliness and worldly lusts, we should live soberly, righteously, and godly in the present age."

Romans 6:12 "Therefore do not let sin reign in your mortal body, that you should obey it in its lusts."

I Peter 2:11 "Beloved, I beg you as sojourners and pilgrims, abstain from fleshly lusts which war against the soul."

36

The fear of the Lord leads to life, and he who has it will abide in satisfaction; he will not be visited with evil. Proverbs 19:23

God wants us to be content. I Timothy 6:6 says, "Now godliness with contentment is great gain." This verse tells us how to have contentment: if we live in the fear of the Lord, we will live in satisfaction, or contentment.

This is contrary to our natural impulse. If we are discontent with a situation in our lives, our first thought is usually to change that situation. It is good and right that we would look forward to certain events: a move to a better house, a husband's job change to a better job, the conception of a baby, the birth of a baby, a new homeschooling curriculum, and all the other things that are so important in our lives. The problem comes when we are not content to wait patiently until the Lord's timing for these events. We grow impatient and anxious, and grumble in our hearts.

Sometimes we are discontent with our situation and there seems no end in sight. Our husbands aren't growing in perfection at the rate that we would like to see them grow, money is tight and getting tighter, the neighbourhood is driving us nuts and there's no opportunity to move......and we sigh and mope and wish things were different.

Did you know that even if you got the thing you craved, it wouldn't make you content? Oh yes, you might be content for a while in that particular area of life, but your heart would soon find something else to be discontent over. Ecclesiastes 5:10 says, "He who loves silver will not be satisfied with silver; nor he who loves abundance, with increase. This also is vanity." I'm sure you've seen a toddler that wants something—a balloon, for example—and will cry with all the ardour of his little heart until he gets it. He is happy and cheerful then, but only for about 15 minutes. Then he sees something else he wants. We do this all our lives, until we learn that contentment is not about our circumstances.

When we have the fear of the Lord, we will be delighting in His will. And if it is His will for us to remain in that tiny mobile home with six children, or remain in a marriage where the husband is not a spiritual leader, or not be pregnant (or be pregnant) for the third year in a row, then we will be happy to be in the place where He has us. Having the fear of the Lord includes being aware of His greatness, His power, His unsearchable wisdom, and unfailing love. When you catch a glimpse of who God really is, you will bow at His feet and willingly worship and submit your life to His plans.

For further study:

I Timothy 6:6-8 "Now godliness with contentment is great gain. For we brought nothing into this world, and it is certain we can carry nothing out. And having food and clothing, with these we shall be content."

Hebrews 13:5 "Let your conduct be without covetousness; be content with such things as you have. For He Himself has said, "I will never leave you nor forsake you.""

Philippians 4:11-13 "Not that I speak in regard to need, for I have learned in whatever state I am to be content: I know how to be abased, and I know how to abound. Everywhere and in all things I have learned both to be full and to be hungry, both to abound and to suffer need. I can do all things through Christ who strengthens me."

37

Better to dwell in a corner of a housetop, than in a house shared with a contentious woman. Proverbs 21:9

Did you know that you can make your family miserable by having to share a house with you? If you are a contentious woman you will drive your family away, at least emotionally and possibly physically. Since none of us wants that, let's examine some characteristics of a contentious woman.

The word contentious can describe a woman who...

- is argumentative
- nags constantly
- is stubborn
- speaks with an irritated tone of voice
- is ready with a quick retort if something displeases her
- uses sharp words to those around her
- is often "on edge"

Do you recognize yourself in any of those descriptions? Would those around you recognize you as contentious?

The Bible is very specific about the damage that a contentious woman does. Proverbs 27:15,16 says that she is not only irritating to be around, but impossible to restrain or tame. Proverbs 19:13, 21:9 and 21:19 imply that your husband would be better off being far away from you if you are contentious. This kind of woman stands in very real danger of driving away her husband, children and even her friends.

If we have a problem in this area, we need to get rid of those characteristics. Of course, the best way to get rid of them is to replace them with righteous attributes. If a contentious woman is one that is easily upset and irritated, then a righteous woman is one who is predictably pleasant and happy. She has a calm spirit and is at peace with those around her. Her speech is wholesome and edifying, and she is humble and teachable.

I will be the first to admit that I am not predictably pleasant, nor do I always display the other virtues in that description. I am working on it, and hopefully I have made some progress, but there is still a long way to go. How do we get to be that way? Here are some practical things you and I can do:

- Pray specifically for the attribute that is lacking in your life
- Confess your sin each time you fail in that area, both to God and to the people you have sinned against
- Memorize Scripture that deals specifically with the sin you are trying to get rid of
- Practice SMILING at those around you, and saying things in a pleasant tone of voice
- Ask a godly woman or your husband to keep you accountable

For further study:

Colossians 3:8-17 "But now you yourselves are to put off all these: anger, wrath, malice, blasphemy, filthy language out of your mouth. Do not lie to one another, since you have put off the old man with his deeds, and have put on the new man who is renewed in knowledge according to the image of Him who created him, where there is neither Greek nor Jew, circumcised nor uncircumcised, barbarian, Scythian, slave nor free, but Christ is all and in all. Therefore, as the elect of God, holy and beloved, put on tender mercies, kindness, humility, meekness, longsuffering; bearing with one another, and forgiving one another, if anyone has a complaint against another, even as Christ forgave you, so you also must do. But above all these things put on love, which is the bond of perfection. And let the peace of God rule in your hearts, to which also you were called in one body; and be thankful. Let the word of Christ dwell in you richly in all wisdom, teaching and admonishing one another in psalms and hymns and spiritual songs, singing with grace in our hearts to the Lord. And whatever you do in word or deed, do all in the name of the Lord Jesus, giving thanks to God the Father through Him.

I Peter 3:4 "Rather let it be the hidden person of the heart, with the incorruptible beauty of a gentle and quiet spirit, which is very precious in the sight of God."

Also recommended: read James 3 (the whole chapter)

38

The sacrifice of the wicked is an abomination to the Lord, but the prayer of the upright is His delight. Proverbs 15:8

Many unbelievers believe that they can keep God happy by doing the occasional good deed. This verse tells us what God thinks of that! But as believers, we can be a delight to our God, simply by praying to Him. You'd think that we would all be eager to pray, spending every free moment in communion with the Lord. However, I know very few people who are content with their prayer life. Somehow it always ends up on the list of things we're trying to improve on!

In the very busy life that most homeschooling moms lead, it is easy to neglect prayer, isn't it? In my own life I have noticed that there are two types of prayer that I need to engage in: focused, thoughtful prayers that cover all the areas the Bible says to pray about, and the minute-by-minute quick prayers for guidance and help throughout the day.

Focused, longer prayers require a mind that is free of distraction, at least for a few moments, and that is difficult to come by for homeschooling moms! But it is so necessary. There are so many things I need to confess, be thankful for, worship God for, and pray for that I will forget most of them if I don't have them written down, and have a chunk of time set aside for doing just that. Many people in the Bible, including Jesus (Mark 1:35) and David (Psalm 5:3), prayed early in the morning. It is certainly a good way of making sure that your prayer time is not pushed aside throughout the day until you're so tired at night that you can't concentrate! And it's a wonderful way to start the day, before the rest of the family is up. There are those of us, though, who don't do so well at thinking clearly early in the morning. I have often tried to pray in the mornings, but usually find myself nodding back off to sleep – even after getting a drink, washing my face, and getting dressed! So for now I have a time in the afternoons when the children are having a quiet time as well. This enables me to pray without interruption at a time when I am able to focus. Find a time that works for you, and then be consistent in praying during that time.

The other kind of prayer that we need in our lives is the short petition for help when we need God's guidance and wisdom. Nothing should be considered too small to bring to His notice.

Lord, help my son right now in his struggle not to be frustrated as he is learning to write his letters.

Lord, please help my husband to have a safe drive home from work today.

Dear God, please give me wisdom as I discipline this child.

Father, help me as I plan this science experiment for tomorrow.

When we pray in this way, it helps us to keep an eternal perspective on the temporal things that fill our lives. It helps us to view all events as coming from the hand of God, and helps make our response to them a godly one.

God is pleased when we bring all things to Him, because it shows that we are depending on Him, and trusting in Him to lead us. Will you purpose to bring delight to God in this way?

For further study:

Ephesians 6:18 "Praying always with all prayer and supplication in the Spirit, being watchful to this end with all perseverance and supplication for all the saints."

James 5:16 "Confess your trespasses to one another, and pray for one another, that you may be healed. The effective, fervent prayer of a righteous man avails much."

Philippians 4:6, 7 "Be anxious for nothing, but in everything by prayer and supplication, with thanksgiving, let your requests be made known to God. And the peace of God, which surpasses all understanding, will guard your hearts and minds through Christ Jesus."

39

There is desirable treasure, and oil in the dwelling of the wise, but a foolish man squanders it. Proverbs 21:20

So many times we think we *need* to have something, and we spend money on it without even thinking or praying about it. Sometimes it takes something really dramatic to show us how little we really do need. One time when our family was living overseas, our washing machine broke and we had no money to get it fixed. I was all for finding a laundromat, but my husband said we should wash our clothes in the bathtub instead. I had never thought you could get clothes clean in just a bathtub! But for months I washed all our clothes in the bathtub, and was surprised at how well it worked. I would have been squandering money by doing washing at the laundromat for all those months when my husband's plan worked for us just fine at that time.

Is there an area where you are spending your family's money unwisely? I have heard women confess that they overspend on eating out, convenience foods, clothes, toys, home decoration, homeschooling stuff, and kitchen gadgets. If this is an area of weakness for you, consider how you can be a better steward of the resources God has given you.

This is not to say, however, that spending money unless absolutely necessary is a sin. If we wanted to be as frugal as was humanly possible, we could do things like make all our food from scratch, always line-dry our clothes, make our own detergents and cleaners, sew all our own clothes from sale fabrics, buy our fruit and vegetables from a farmer's market, make up our own homeschooling curriculum (to save money on the packaged kind), not use the air conditioning or heating in the house... and the list is nearly endless.

However, if we did all these things, we would hardly be able to do anything else! Making up your own homeschooling curriculum is very time-consuming, and then when would we have the time to grind our own wheat, sew our own clothes, and so on? We must decide what our priorities are, based on what God is requiring from our family, and from there make decisions about what is worth spending money on.

Once a family has decided what their priorities are, they should then see how they can be good stewards within their time and energy constraints. It may well be worth it for a tired, pregnant mom with young children to use paper plates and plastic utensils at lunchtimes, to cut down the time and energy spent washing dishes. If she has enough money to do this, she need not feel guilty! Stewardship is about using resources wisely, not just about saving money.

May God make us prudent women who can discern between needs and wants, and be good stewards of the resources He has given us!

For further study:

Proverbs 8:12 "I, wisdom, dwell with prudence, and find out knowledge and discretion."

Psalm 112:5 "A good man deals graciously and lends; he will guide his affairs with discretion."

40

The lazy man will not plow because of winter; he will beg during harvest and have nothing. Proverbs 20:4

Have you ever noticed that lazy people are expert at making excuses? I am dead lazy by nature, and can think up an excuse for anything that I don't want to do. The sad thing is that I can be taken in by my own excuses, and feel that I don't really deserve the natural consequences of my laziness.

Most lazy people are like me. The excuse given in this verse in Proverbs is typical. The lazy man thinks he can't plow because it's cold outside. It's not convenient for him to work—it would be a hardship—and so the plowing doesn't get done. Other lazy people make up excuses that are so lame that no one would take them seriously. For example, a lazy man described in Proverbs 22:13 says that he can't go to work because there might be a lion in the streets that would kill him! This excuse could only appear reasonable to a fool, and that's what the Bible says: "The lazy man is wiser in his own eyes than seven men who can answer sensibly." (Proverbs 26:7)

What sort of excuses do you make when you are feeling lazy? Are you waiting for a more convenient time to do something? Do you tell yourself that there's a risk in doing this particular thing? (Even though it's a risk you would think nothing of if you really wanted to do this thing.) Are you just "too tired" to do it now? The sort of rest that a lazy person uses to avoid working is not the kind of rest that brings refreshment. It is the sort that leads to more laziness: "Laziness casts one into a deep sleep, and an idle person will suffer hunger" (Proverbs 19:15).

Now, there are times when we simply cannot work, and there is a valid reason. Another passage in Proverbs deals with excuse-making. When God asks His people to deliver others from danger, and the excuse given is that they didn't know what was happening, the writer of this Proverb says, "Does not He who weighs the hearts consider it? He who keeps your soul, does He not know it? And will He not render to each man according to his deeds?" (Proverbs 24:12). God is the one that will determine if your excuse is valid or not. Most of the time, when I examine my own excuses ("I can't organize my bedroom yet because I'm waiting to get those special baskets to put things in") they are pretty pathetic. May God help us to look at our excuses through His eyes, and make us honest with ourselves.

James 1:24, 25 "For he observes himself, goes away, and immediately forgets what kind of man he was. But he who looks into the perfect law of liberty and continues in it, and is not a forgetful hearer but a doer of the work, this one will be blessed in what he does."

Ecclesiastes 4:5 "The fool folds his hand and consumes his own flesh."

41

A prudent man conceals knowledge, but the heart of fools proclaims foolishness.
Proverbs 12:23

All of us who are homeschooling are teachers. Some of us may have a natural giftedness for teaching, or we may have at one time been teachers in a setting other than our home. Whatever our background, teaching sometimes gets into the blood. Whatever knowledge we possess we long to pass on to someone else. We hate to see incorrect information and cannot be silent until the mistake is corrected. All this is very good when we are teaching our children. It is not so good when we give this impulse free reign in our other relationships.

When your husband makes a statement that you feel is incorrect, do you jump on it immediately with a correction? If a friend gives her theory about something and you disagree, do you take it upon yourself to enlighten her then and there? There are some issues that are so serious that they may require an immediate statement from you. But the vast majority of things that we feel we need to share are not in that category.

If you have found a method of doing something (housecleaning, child training, homeschooling....) that works very well for you, don't burden everyone around you with your knowledge. To be prudent, as this verse says, you need to consider what is appropriate to say and what isn't. What you have to say may very well be true and helpful. But it may not be the time and place to say it. At the right time and place, our words may be a welcome help to someone who needs the knowledge that you have. But you must be discerning about when you should share.

As this verse says, when we are in the habit of proclaiming what we think is true knowledge, we will inevitably spout foolishness, at least some of the time. How many of your theories and methods have changed over the years? The older you are and the more children you have, the more your mind will probably have changed about some things! Some of what you used to believe evidently wasn't "the answer" you once thought it was. So rather than spend a lot of time and energy proclaiming things that you may one day change your mind about, be wise and "conceal" your knowledge unless you know that you should speak.

For further study:

I Corinthians 8:1 "Now concerning things offered to idols: we know that we all have knowledge. Knowledge puffs up, but love edifies."

I Samuel 2:3 "Talk no more so very proudly; let no arrogance come from your mouth, for the Lord is the God of knowledge; and by Him actions are weighed."

Romans 12:16 "Be of the same mind toward one another. Do not set your mind on high things, but associate with the humble. Do not be wise in your own opinion."

42

He who gathers in summer is a wise son; He who sleeps in harvest is a son who causes shame. Proverbs 10:5

Notice that the verse isn't condemning general laziness, but a particular kind. Our family lives in rural Ireland, and there is a definite harvest time each year. At the end of summer, the farmers become extremely busy, harvesting crops, hay, and silage. When the older generation are sitting around telling stories about colourful characters in the area, I have heard stories told of farmers who were lazy and didn't get the hay baled in time, and it was ruined. The stories are told in a funny way, and everyone laughs, but it's clear that these farmers are not respected. When it is harvest time, you may not feel like going out and working. But if you don't, what should have been harvested will be wasted, and you will lose money.

We mothers can apply this verse in two ways. The first way is to recognize that our children need to be trained to work diligently. Do you want children of whom you will be ashamed? Nobody does! But you will, unless you teach them to work diligently. Schoolwork, chores, and music practice are typical scheduled activities that require our children to work hard. What if they don't feel like doing piano practice when they should? What if they don't want to empty the trash right now? When you let them put off their tasks until they feel like doing them, you are in effect training them to sleep during harvest, and thus storing up shame for yourself. You need to hold them to the assigned task when it is scheduled, and then they will learn to do what they should when they should, regardless of their feelings. What a blessing this will be to them throughout their lives!

The other application is to ourselves. We need to train ourselves, if we have never been taught, to do what we should when we should, regardless of our feelings. If we are lazy in this way, we will bring shame to our families—especially to our husbands. Proverbs 12:4 says that a wife who causes shame is like rottenness in her husband's bones. I'm sure that thought is repellent to every Christian wife! So let's ask God to make us women who won't sleep during the harvest time.

I Timothy 5:9, 10 "Do not let a widow under sixty years old be taken into the number, and not unless she has been the wife of one man, well reported for good works: if she has brought up children, if she has lodged strangers, if she has washed the saints' feet, if she has relieved the afflicted, if she has diligently followed every good work."

Galatians 6:9 "And let us not grow weary while doing good, for in due season we shall reap if we do not lose heart."

I Thessalonians 4:11, 12 "That you also aspire to lead a quiet life, to mind your own business, and to work with your own hands as we commanded you, that you may walk properly toward those who are outside, and that you may lack nothing."

43

Better is a dinner of herbs where love is, than a fatted calf with hatred. Proverbs 15:17

When I was first married, I was talking to a friend who was also a newlywed. She was describing their home life, and she said in passing, "Our home is really filled with so much love." That phrase has stuck with me through the years as the ideal description of a Christian home. A house filled with love; isn't there something enticing even in the sound of that? "A house filled with expensive items" isn't nearly so attractive.

Of course this verse is speaking generally about how superior love is to riches, but it also alludes directly to food—or to put it in modern terms, the dinner table. How much of an effort do you make to have the dinner table be a place of love? Do you put as much energy into that as you do into fixing the food? In many homes, especially those with young children, the dinner table often turns into merely a time of directives from the parents to the children: "Don't put that glass there—you'll knock it over." "Don't talk with your mouth full." "Please eat all the green beans on your plate.' "Don't tap the table with your spoon—ok, with your fork." And so on. As parents we might get increasingly irritated with the number of small infractions and end by saying in a disgusted voice, "Well, you just lost the chance of any dessert!" And in between these instructions to the children, the parents try to communicate important information about what the dentist said or what's wrong with the washing machine. It's not a very pleasant picture, is it?

Well, I don't have a solution that will instantly solve the problem, but here are some thoughts on making meals a little more laced with love.

- Really work on table manners at breakfast and lunch, so that not so much correction will be required at dinner.
- Plan out in advance edifying topics that the family could discuss during dinner. When I was young, our family went around the table and each shared what we were thankful for that day. You could also talk through a situation and decide what a biblical response would be.
- Pray as you are preparing the food, that this meal would bring glory to God.
- Help the children think through in advance something they would like to share with Dad about their day, or a question they would like to ask him.

So often children spout foolishness because they haven't been directed to say anything worthwhile.

Love makes the most humble, plain food into a feast. Wouldn't you like to give your family a feast every day?

For further study:

Proverbs 17:1 "Better is a dry morsel with quietness, than a house full of feasting with strife."

I Corinthians 10:31 "Therefore, whether you eat or drink, or whatever you do, do all to the glory of God."

44

He who covers a transgression seeks love, but he who repeats a matter separates friends.
Proverbs 17:9

I Peter 4:8 echoes what this proverb is saying when it tells us that "love will cover a multitude of sins." Real Christian love will overlook many a fault, and forbear with other people's wrongs and mistakes.

But it's all too tempting in our families to "repeat a matter," isn't it? I have often forgiven my husband for some little wrong he has done me, but then bring it up again weeks later. With our children, too, we can recall with complete clarity every instance of irresponsibility that we have seen in them since they were in diapers, and prove it by narrating it all to them when they make another childish mistake. What's worse, we might even tell other people about the faults our husband or children have, even after we have said we forgive them.

There may be times in dealing with a pattern of sin in someone else, and giving them a loving, biblical rebuke, that you are forced to give examples to them of the times they have committed this sin. That is not wrong—in fact, it is much better than saying, "You have a problem with pride" and expecting them to take your word for it.

However, the majority of times that we bring up past wrongs, especially with our husbands, it is because we are still bothered by what they did and don't want them to forget how they made us suffer. This Proverb tells us what will happen if we do this. If such behaviour separates friends, it certainly will drive a wedge between us and our spouse! Who would want to live with someone who was always reminding them of their defeats and failures? The Bible tells us to forget what lies behind and press on toward the goal of godliness (Philippians 3:13, 14), and we make that hard for those around us if we won't allow them to forget!

If you have this problem, think about what motivates you to bring up past sins again. Is it a desire for a bit of subtle revenge? Is it bitterness because you didn't really forgive the person when they asked you to? Real, fervent love will keep this from happening. Realize the destructive nature of repeating a matter, and ask God to help you show it in the way you forgive.

Proverbs 10:12 "Hatred stirs up strife, but love covers all sins."

Philippians 2:1-4 "Therefore, if there is any consolation in Christ, if any comfort of love, if any fellowship of the Spirit, if any affection and mercy, fulfill my joy by being like-minded, having the same love, being of one accord, of one mind. Let nothing be done through selfish ambition or conceit, but in lowliness of mind let each esteem others better than himself. Let each of you look out not only for his own interests, but also for the interests of others."

Matthew 18:21, 22 "Then Peter came up to Him and said, 'Lord, how often shall my brother sin against me, and I forgive him? Up to seven times?' Jesus said to him, 'I do not say to you, up to seven times, but up to seventy times seven.'"

45

The fear of the Lord is the beginning of wisdom, and the knowledge of the Holy One is understanding. Proverbs 9:10

I attended a particular Christian school for the first six years of my school life. Every morning, each class would recite Proverbs 9:10 in unison. Having repeated it thousands of times throughout my childhood, this verse is ingrained on my mind, and I am so thankful that it is because it holds such great truth! For us mothers who are responsible for the day-to-day education and training of our children, it gives us direction and focus.

The Hebrew concept of wisdom was not associated with an accumulation of knowledge. It had more to do with having skill in the art of living. It should be the goal of our parenting to produce wise children—children who are skilled at living. This verse tells us where to start in producing these children: the fear of the Lord.

As you may know, "fear" here means a reverential awe of God, not a spooky kind of fear. This fear comes by knowing who He is, as it says in the second part of the verse. If we meditate on the attributes of God, especially the ones that we can't imitate, we will begin to have a reverence for our God. Think of His power in creation, His sovereignty, His omnipotence (He is all-powerful), His omniscience (He is all-knowing), and His eternality.

Fearing God, though, is more than just an attitude. In the Bible, one who fears God is one whose life is pleasing to God. If we truly fear God, we will obey Him. Then, the Bible says, we will be wise and have understanding. Do we show our children the mighty, awe-inspiring attributes of God in the way we teach them? Or do we constantly emphasize God's love and mercy to the exclusion of all other characteristics?

We can train our children into good behaviour while they are under our care, but unless they fear God they will not truly have wisdom as they grow up and leave home. May we honor the Lord in our presentation of His character to our children.

For further study:

Jeremiah 32:39-40 "Then I will give them one heart and one way, that they may fear Me forever, for the good of them and their children after them. And I will make an everlasting covenant with them, that I will not turn away from doing them good; but I will put My fear in their hearts so that they will not depart from Me."

Proverbs 8:13 "The fear of the Lord is to hate evil: pride and arrogance and the evil way and the perverse mouth I hate."

I Samuel 12:24 "Only fear the Lord, and serve Him in truth with all your heart; for consider what great things He has done for you."

Hebrews 12:28, 29 "Therefore, since we are receiving a kingdom which cannot be shaken, let us have grace, by which we may serve God acceptably with reverence and godly fear. For our God is a consuming fire."

46

He who covers his sins will not prosper, but whoever confesses and forsakes them will have mercy. Proverbs 28:13

Do you try to cover up your sins so that your family won't know? See if any of these sound familiar:

- Hiding your gluttony by concealing sweet treats and then indulging yourself when no one is around
- Deliberately not telling your husband that you bought something when you know he would have preferred you not to get it
- Acting like you forgot to do something when actually you just chose not to do it
- Exaggerating how tired or sick you feel so that you can be excused for not keeping up with your duties

And I'm sure you could think of many more. Proverbs says that the one who does these kinds of things will not prosper. A Christian cannot sin successfully! You will feel continual guilt, and God will keep after you — perhaps even chastise you — until you repent.

On the other hand, one who makes a habit of confessing wrongdoing, and proves their sincerity by changing their behaviour, will find mercy from the God who pardons them. Are you in the *habit* of confession? Do you apologize immediately to your children when your voice is raised in irritation with them? When you forget to keep a promise you made, do you humbly ask their forgiveness? Do you seek the forgiveness of your husband when you fail to do as he asked you to? If so, then you will find it much easier to keep a clear conscience all of the time.

The truth is that our sin is already covered, by the grace of God. Psalm 85:2 says, "You have forgiven the iniquity of Your people; You have covered all their sin." When the Lord has covered over our sin and doesn't remember it any more, then why should we be concealing it and suffering under guilt and the fear of being found out? When we confess our sin, we give glory to God (Joshua 7:19).

God does not need us to confess for His own information, but He commands it because it is for our good. Those of us who are at home all day every day with family members will sin against them many times every week, if not every day.

Will you take the opportunities God has given you to practice confessing and forsaking your sin?

For further study:

James 5:16 "Confess your trespasses to one another, and pray for one another, that you may be healed. The effective, fervent prayer of a righteous man avails much."

Psalm 32:1 "Blessed is he whose transgression is forgiven, whose sin is covered."

Jeremiah 3:13 "Only acknowledge your iniquity, that you have transgressed against the Lord your God, and have scattered your charms to alien deities under every green tree, and you have not obeyed My voice,' says the Lord."

47

He who trusts in his own heart is a fool, but whoever walks wisely will be delivered.
Proverbs 28:26

Our hearts are the most untrustworthy advisors. The prophet Jeremiah tells us that our hearts are deceitful above all things and desperately wicked (Jeremiah 17:9). We know from experience that they have led us wrong before. That doesn't always stop us, though, from listening to those little traitors.

Perhaps we have imbibed a bit of the world's philosophy that tells us that to find direction for our lives, we need to follow our hearts. Rich Mullins, in his song "The Maker of Noses," describes it this way: "They said, 'Boy, you just follow your heart,' but my heart just led me into my chest." Following your heart won't get you anywhere good.

How do you know if you are trusting in your own heart?

- If you believe that you have within yourself the resources to live a godly life ("I would *never* fall into a sin like adultery!"
- If you are brimming with self-confidence about your abilities and skills ("I'm so glad I have it all together in the area of keeping a clean and comfortable home.")
- If you believe that in this or that small area you don't have to do exactly what the Bible says ("I know it says that 'bad company corrupts good character,' but it's not going to hurt me just to have this one friend who's a bit on the wild side…")
- If you allow yourself access to things you know you will be addicted to ("It's ok, I know what I'm doing; I can handle it.")
- If you believe that homeschooling mothers are somehow automatically exempt from committing any big, terrible sins. ("I'm so sheltered that I'm never even within the reach of temptation!")

Someone who is truly wise will be *afraid* of trusting in their own heart. They will do what God's Word says regardless of what their heart is telling them to do. Do you remember the story of the wise man who built on the rock? Jesus said he was the one who heard Jesus' words and obeyed them. "And the rain descended, the floods came, and the winds blew and beat on that house; and it did not fall, for it was founded on the rock" (Matt. 7:25). But contrast this with the man who trusted in himself—he heard Jesus' words and did not do them, which was like building a house on the sand. And when the storm came, "the house fell, and great was its fall" (Matt. 7: 27).

Building your life on the foundation of your own heart will produce a very shaky structure! Renounce your own heart as the great pretender that it is, and walk in wisdom and the fear of the Lord.

For further study:

Psalm 118:8, 9 "It is better to trust in the Lord than to put confidence in man. It is better to trust in the Lord than to put confidence in princes."

Psalm 25:20 "Keep my soul, and deliver me; let me not be ashamed, for I put my trust in You."

Philippians 3:3, 4 "For we are the circumcision, who worship God in the Spirit, rejoice in Christ Jesus, and have no confidence in the flesh, though I also might have confidence in the flesh. If anyone else thinks he may have confidence in the flesh, I more so."

Isaiah 57:13 "When you cry out, let your collection of idols deliver you. But the wind will carry them all away, a breath will take them. But he who puts his trust in Me shall possess the land, and shall inherit my holy mountain."

48

The wise in heart will be called prudent, and sweetness of the lips increases learning.
Proverbs 16:21

When my husband was growing up in Ireland, teachers were not known for their sweetness of speech. If a child couldn't read something correctly, the teacher might say, "You're blind as well as stupid!" And they would ridicule the students for their mistakes, often telling them that they would never amount to anything in society. Thankfully, this no longer happens in Irish schools. But many people grew up feeling stupid and loathing formal learning because of they way they were taught when they were young.

As homeschooling mothers, we are the primary teachers in our children's lives. Not only are we their teachers academically, but we probably give them more instruction than anyone else does on how to do housework and chores, how to get along with each other, and how to accomplish those life skills that they will need as adults. Of course, biblically all these things are directed by the father of the family, and you are only teaching these things under his direction. But you probably do most of the actual teaching and training, since you are with the children the most.

This proverb says that our children will learn more if we speak sweetly as we are instructing them. If we are full of encouragement and enthusiasm, they will understand and retain so much more than if we sound bored, irritated, or even angry. In my life I have spent twenty years in school, and the information I learned best was taught by the teachers who were encouraging and excited about the lessons.

This goes beyond just schooling. As we are training our children to remember to close the screen door, to wipe their muddy boots before coming in, or to pick up the toys they left scattered, we will accomplish our goal more quickly if we use kind, sweet words than if we holler, "Close that screen door!!" If someone is exasperated with you or yells at you, stubbornness rises in your heart, doesn't it? Do you really feel like taking to heart what the person is trying to teach you when instructions are given in a harsh way?

Let's make it easy for our children to learn from us by using the kind of words God is pleased with.

For further study:

Proverbs 16:24 "Pleasant words are like a honeycomb, sweetness to the soul and health to the bones."

Ephesians 4:29 "Let no corrupt word proceed out of your moth, but what is good for necessary edification, that it may impart grace to the hearers."

Colossians 4:6 "Let your speech always be with grace, seasoned with salt, that you may know how you ought to answer each one."

49

Whoever has no rule over his own spirit is like a city broken down, without walls.
Proverbs 25:28

In our family, one of the first lessons we try to teach our children is that of self-control. Self-control is a foundational virtue — without it, it will be impossible for you to do what is right when you don't feel like it. Without self control, a person will succumb to every temptation, just like a city without walls is open to every invader.

I have often been convicted in my own life that I expect so much self-control from even a toddler, while I myself don't always rule over my own spirit. I find myself getting vexed when the children keep interrupting with questions while I'm trying to read aloud to them, or when I have to stop dinner preparations to discipline a child. I am memorizing Proverbs 16:32 to remind me how to respond in these situations: "He who is slow to anger is better than the mighty, and he who rules his spirit than he who takes a city." If you can conquer *yourself*, you are better than one who conquers a whole city!

Of course we need self control in the face of all temptations, not just anger. Our battles against laziness, gossip, gluttony, lying, boasting, selfishness, and so on all require self-mastery for victory. Whenever we do what we should do in the face of contrary emotions, that is showing self-control. But we must be careful not to put confidence in our self-control to keep us from sin. Romans 6:14 says, "For sin shall not have dominion over you, for you are not under law but under grace." It is the grace of God that gives us the power to rule our own spirit. Before we were Christians, we had no choice but to sin. Sin dominated our lives and we were slaves to it (Romans 6:6). But now by grace we have been set free from the law of sin and death (Romans 8:2) and we can chose to do right.

We need to take the opportunities we have every day for instilling this virtue in both our children and ourselves. The benefits are numerous, and eternal.

For further study:

I Corinthians 9:25 "And everyone who competes for the prize is temperate in all things. Now they do it to obtain a perishable crown, but we for an imperishable crown."

Galatians 5:23 "[but the fruit of the spirit is] gentleness and self-control."

I Peter 1:13 "Therefore gird up the loins of your mind, be sober, and rest your hope fully upon the grace that is to be brought to you at the revelation of Jesus Christ."

2 Peter 1:5, 6 "But also for this very reason, giving all diligence, add to your faith virtue, to virtue knowledge, to knowledge self-control, to self-control perseverance, to perseverance godliness"

50

In all your ways acknowledge Him, and He shall direct your paths. Proverbs 3:6

This verse says that we are to acknowledge God in all our ways. This means that even in the ordinary matters of everyday life, God loves to be consulted. The nineteenth century Bible commentator Charles Bridges says this about this verse: "Be in the habit of going to him *in the first place* — before self-will, self-pleasing, self-wisdom, human friends, convenience, expediency. Before any of these have been consulted go to God at once. Consider no circumstances too clear to need his direction." (Bridges, Charles *Proverbs*, Banner of Truth Trust, 1968, p. 24.)

There is an attitude of submission to God in all of this. We take all our ways to God for His approval, direction, and wisdom, and then we do His will in all these things. We follow where He leads without trying to arrange our lives the way *we* think they ought to go.

Then the verse says that God will direct our paths. Really, the promise that He will do this is dependant on the three conditions preceding it: that we trust in the Lord with all our hearts, that we do not lean on our own understanding, and that we acknowledge Him in all our ways. But what does it mean that God directs our path? Literally, the Hebrew says that He will make the way smooth or straight. Does this mean that we will have an easy life? No. For one thing, we know that "all who desire to live godly in Christ Jesus will be persecuted" (2 Tim. 3:12). And James tells us that we are to "count it all joy when we encounter various trials," which assumes that we will be having trials.

So what does it mean that God will make our way straight? It means that he will clear the way for us, to break a path, as it were. He will go before us and make clear the path that we are to go on. And our path *will* be easier than if we didn't follow God. So often we hear of unbelieving families who follow worldly wisdom and their lives are in chaos. Sometimes the lives of the wicked do seem smooth and easy, as Asaph thought (Psalm 73). But in that Psalm we see that even those whose lives appear to be happy are just about to hit calamity. Therefore, we can believe God that if we follow His ways, He will indeed make our paths straight.

Proverbs 3:21-26 "My son, let them not depart from your eyes—keep sound wisdom and discretion; so they will be life to your soul and grace to your neck. Then you will walk safely in your way, and your foot will not stumble. When you lie down, you will not be afraid; yes, you will lie down and your sleep will be sweet. Do not be afraid of sudden terror, nor of trouble from the wicked when it comes; for the Lord will be your confidence, and will keep your foot from being caught."

Psalm 32:10 "Many sorrows shall be to the wicked; but he who trusts in the Lord, mercy shall surround him."

Psalm 37:5 "Commit your way to the Lord, trust also in Him, and He shall bring it to pass."

Made in the USA
Lexington, KY
29 April 2015